Recipes from a
Provençal Kitchen

Michel Biehn

Recipes from a Provençal Kitchen

Photography
by Bernard Touillon

~

Translated by
Antony & Christine Grant

Flammarion
Paris - New York

For Paul and Jeanne

Originally published in 1994 by Flammarion
as *Le Cahier de Recettes Provençales*
English translation copyright © Reed Consumer Books
Translated by Antony & Christine Grant
U.S. consultants: Jenni Fleetwood, Stephanie Driver

Editorial Direction:
Ghislaine Bavoillot

Designed by Marc Walter
Color separation by Colourscan France
Typesetting by Dorchester Typesetting Group Ltd
Printed and bound in Italy by G. Canale & C. S.p.A.

ISBN: 2-08015-679-8
Numéro d'édition: FA 3679/09
Dépôt légal: March 1995

Flammarion
26, rue Racine
75006 Paris

c o n t e n t s

— 7 —
THE SIMPLICITY OF
MY GRANDMOTHER'S COOKING

— 17 —
AUTUMN SQUASH

— 35 —
CABBAGE AND ROMANCE

— 45 —
TEATIME IN THE KITCHEN

— 59 —
A CHRISTMAS SUPPER IN PROVENCE

— 71 —
FROM CHRISTMAS TO NEW YEAR

— 77 —
UNDER A WINTER'S SUN

— 93 —
A SPRING LUNCH

— 111 —
BREAKFAST WITH THE HORSEMEN

— 123 —
BOUILLABAISSE
IN AN ARTIST'S STUDIO

— 139 —
A PICNIC ON THE BANKS OF THE
RIVER SORGUE

— 151 —
A DAY AT THE "CABANON"

— 167 —
LUNCH ON THE TERRACE

— 183 —
A GARDEN FEAST

THE SIMPLICITY OF MY GRANDMOTHER'S COOKING

Like my father I have always loved food. When my parents were married in 1947 in Arles, my grandmother, Athalie Pascal, armed with ink and pen, copied into a school notebook the recipes she had learned from her own mother. In another book were inscribed her pastry and dessert recipes. She gave these books to her daughter on her wedding day, as she had done for my Uncle Victor and my Aunt Elisabeth a few years earlier. I have those notebooks with me now and many of the recipes in this book, the added touches, a "small carrot" here, a "sprig of thyme" there, come from the subtle *savoir-faire* of that beautiful and generous woman, brought up in Sault, who was my grandmother.

My mother very quickly added her own personal touches to the notebook recipes. This delighted her husband, her son, and her friends, for she developed a style of cooking that was both simple and refined, in the Provençal tradition, but also quite often enriched with butter and cream, which my father loved, for he was from Alsace. I was often in the kitchen with my mother. I loved watching her work, and from time to time, she even let me help.

As a child, one of my great joys on Christmas Eve was to prepare the almonds for the Yule log. It was a task I undertook almost religiously. First, I had to break the shells, then blanch the nuts in a pan of boiling water. Next I skinned the nuts and dried them in a cloth. I spread them in a small metal dish which had two brass handles. The dish went into a low oven where the almonds were roasted until golden, but not burned. Then, while they were still hot, I would place them between two sheets of thick paper, and with all my might I would crush them into a powder with a rolling pin. There is nothing I remember with greater pleasure than the aroma rising from the nuts at that moment.

Athalie Pascal's recipe notebook

Now I, too, have filled a notebook with recipes, a large white book covered in cloth embroidered with blue and yellow silks, bought at the flea market. In it, over the years, I have recorded the exotic culinary discoveries of my friends, and the memories of all the meals shared with the people dear to me. They have shaped my love of good food, and considerably added to my own knowledge of cooking.

In Arles, in the old days, when a woman was in her everyday clothes, she was said to be in a dress of "simplicity" as compared to the more elaborate one worn on Sundays. In the same way, one can think of Provençal cooking as *une cuisine de simplicité*. If in Provence we cook elaborate dishes prepared with puff pastry, sauces, and mousses, we are not being true to the Provençal tradition. This is *la cuisine bourgeoise*, "as found in Paris." Provençal cooking derives its original flavors from the marvelous products either grown, raised, or found in Provence or near its coasts: the anchovies and *tellines* (our own brand of cockles), the cardoons and purple artichokes, garlic and olives, almonds and truffles. Cooking techniques are mainly simple: broiling, baking, and boiling are the methods used, with a few simmered dishes such as *daube* and *barigoule*. The only sauces used are *coulis de tomates*, *rouille*, and *aïoli*, and,

more often than not, just a dash of olive oil. For dessert, some fresh *brousse* cheese with jam, or simply fruit, since we believe that Provence grows the most beautiful fruit on earth.

Provençal cooking is also seasonal cooking, using fresh ingredients bought from the market when they are in their prime. Zucchini are best in the summer and asparagus at Easter time. No cans, except for tomatoes, because when you have to make a tomato *coulis* in December, canned tomatoes are preferable to those anemic and tasteless greenhouse tomatoes for which you pay a fortune.

What makes this cuisine unique and subtle is the refined, artistic, almost scientific way the people of Provence have of enhancing flavors with vegetables, herbs, and spices, and of blending them together. For example the leek, when it is not used as a main vegetable in a dish, is often added for flavor in small quantities to fish recipes, especially salt cod. This is equally true of carrots and olives in recipes for meat stews. Anchovies also play an important role in many dishes and they enhance beautifully the flavor of our Easter leg of kid, as well as that of a Christmas cardoon gratin.

Above all, it is my mission to refute the heresy that *herbes de Provence* are the basic flavors of Provence. Cooking *à la*

Flowering thyme

provençale does not mean dipping into a big bag of mixed herbs and throwing them onto broiled meats and roasts, or into sauces or stews. That is an old wives' tale. But a sprig of thyme, a bay leaf, or a piece of orange rind, sometimes together, sometimes separate, will definitely flavor a *daube* or a *coulis* in the traditional Provençal way.

There is one more ingredient which deserves a special mention and that is shredded cheese. In Provence, we just call it *le râpé*. We serve it with all the soups and it covers most gratins, with or without breadcrumbs. In the past, Dutch cheese was used, which we used to call *le rouge* (Dutch Edam with annatto coloring)—then Gruyère arrived and completely replaced *le rouge*. I personally think that it is a pity and that we should go back to the old ways and use *le rouge* on *soupe au pistou*, for instance.

As we have talked about cheese, I would like to say a few words about our bread. Everywhere in Provence, the bread is excellent and our bakers are true artists. They have the know-how to create a great variety of shapes and textures, and they have given them lovely names like *l'épi* (ear of corn) and *le fendu* (split), *la couronne* (wreath) and *la fougasse, le pain d'Aix* and *le petit Beaucaire*.

Of course, I must also mention the delicious wines of Provence—the *rosés* of Palette and Bandol, of Ventoux and the Luberon—that one drinks chilled in the summer. We also have superb reds from Gigondas and Aix-en-Provence and white from Cassis and Châteauneuf-du-Pape, not to mention the muscat from Beaumes-de-Venise. Every time it seemed appropriate, I have suggested one of these wines to accompany the recipes in this book.

As you will have guessed by now, I love this part of the world, its food and its customs, and I hope you will want to share that passion. But as I have already told you, my father was from Alsace, and a lover of good food, and I must admit that his influence has slightly subverted an otherwise fairly strict family tradition when it comes to cooking. So do not be surprised if my dessert and pastry recipes seem a little richer than Provençal simplicity would usually allow. Apart from these few exceptions, and some exotic inclusions suggested by friends, I do try to be a faithful follower of that beautiful Provençal tradition. Nevertheless, this book does not pretend to be an exhaustive, historical or ethnological study of the culinary habits and customs of Provençal cooks, nor is it an instruction manual, so that although you will find all the details

"Le râpé"

Pages 12-13: Athalie Pascal's recipe notebook

necessary to prepare the recipes, I have not included a list of ingredients, nor have I organized the recipes by type.

This book is first and foremost a gathering of friends. I wanted to take you on a gourmet tour of a house, a dream house which would have a terrace overlooking the sea, as well as a garden on the banks of the River Sorgue, a big yellow living room and a small red drawing room, a spiral staircase going up to the attic, a stately kitchen and a vegetable garden, a window opening onto the Camargue and another onto Mount Ventoux.

In welcoming me into their homes, my friends have allowed me to make this

"Le rouge"

dream house come true. So, we will go to the Château de l'Ange in Lumières, the house of Michel and Edith Mézard, for a candlelit dinner for two and a garden feast. The afternoon tea will be served in the kitchen of the Château d'Ansouis, the home of Géraud and Stéphanette de Sabran-Pontèves. We will celebrate Christmas at Vinsobres, at Jean and Hélène Feraud's house. Lillian Williams will let us lunch with the Chinese mandarins in the main living room of her *bastide* near Aix-en-Provence. Jack Grange will welcome us into his garden overlooking the Alpille Hills. Then we'll share lunch with *les gardians* (horsemen) in the heart of the Camargue at Henri, Annie, and Patrick Laurent's *mas des Marquises*. We'll spend a day in a creek, at Denis Savon's *cabanon*. Finally, we'll dine under Bruno Carles' veranda at Lunel, and Gérard Drouillet will prepare a *bouillabaisse* in his studio in Eygalières. For each of these magical places, I have chosen a special time of year and I have organized the recipes in Athalie's notebook according to the passing of the seasons.

This book is a very personal vision of the simple and beautiful way in which the people of Provence enjoy each other's company. It makes each moment of life happy, and in perfect harmony with the climate, the countryside, and the special light of Provence.

Breads from Provence: "L'épi" and le fendu, la fougasse, le pain d'Aix and le petit Beaucaire"

A UTUMN S QUASH

It is fall in Provence. The tourists, a little sad, are going home and our village squares have stopped being ugly parking lots and returned to their usual peace and quiet. Summer lingers on, the air is exquisitely mild, and the light, oblique and clear, is more beautiful than ever. Still, the leaves are falling from the trees and the days are shorter. The garden is turning yellow with the lime trees and red with the ripening persimmons. In the morning, after the mist has lifted, one can pick the last tomatoes, the ones that will never ripen, with which to make jam. In the pine trees the *cigales* (cicadas) have stopped singing until next summer, while on the kitchen walls, their well-behaved ceramic cousins seem to enjoy the aromas coming from a pumpkin transformed into a lovely soup tureen and filled with a delicious thick bread soup, or those from the large green cabbage which has been stuffed and re-formed into its beautiful rounded shape. In the oven, the pieces of rabbit in mustard sauce are roasting nicely. The crusts are forming on the gratins, and the potatoes are turning plump and golden. On a baking sheet, the candied orange and lemon rinds are drying along with the large sheets of quince paste. Meanwhile, soft chocolate fudge is hardening on a marble slab before being wrapped in silver paper. It is fall in our kitchen at l'Isle-sur-la-Sorgue. Welcome.

*Pumpkin
and Bread
Soup*

*Pages 18-19:
The kitchen
with cicadas*

Pumpkin and
Bread Soup

~

The pumpkin we grow around here is called "nutmeg" pumpkin. Its rind is a milky caramel color—less red than American pumpkin—its flesh a bright orange, sweet and full of flavor. In the pumpkin family it is rather small, much smaller than the celebrated pumpkin which, on fairytale nights, is transformed into Cinderella's carriage. We harvest pumpkins in the fall, and, as with apples, as long as they are unblemished they keep all winter.

Here is a beautiful soup, one in which the pumpkin will play all the parts: the soup tureen and the soup, the dish and the meal, the decanter and the wine. Don't laugh, wait until you've tried it!

IN THE KITCHEN : Choose a nice unblemished pumpkin, weighing 6 to 8 pounds. Cut out a lid in the top—a large hole—through which a ladle can pass easily. With a spoon, remove and discard all the seeds and the fibers surrounding them. Fill the inside of the pumpkin with small cubes of dry bread and shredded cheese, salt and pepper, and 1 or 2 garlic cloves, finely chopped. Then pour in some fairly liquid heavy cream—enough to cover the bread—to about an inch from the top. Put the lid back on the pumpkin, wrap it in aluminum foil and bake for 2 hours in a preheated oven at 375°.

Taking the pumpkin out of the oven can be tricky because the skin will have softened during cooking. Be careful not to let it collapse. Remove the foil and let the pumpkin drain for a while. Then put it in a deep dish and remove the lid. With a wooden spoon, carefully scrape away the cooked flesh, not too close to the skin, and mix it with the cream and bread. For a smooth soup, the mixture can be puréed. Ladle this thick and delicious soup into warmed bowls.

Stuffed Pumpkin

~

For this recipe you will need a small pumpkin, about 8 inches in diameter. Cut out a lid in the top and remove and discard the seeds and the fibers surrounding them. Using a spoon, scoop out the flesh. You will need only about half of it—the remainder can go into a vegetable soup. Chop up the flesh with 2 garlic cloves and a generous bunch of parsley, and then fry in olive oil until well cooked; season with salt, pepper, and a pinch of sugar. Chop up 1 pound of leftover cooked meat (beef, pork, or lamb will do nicely) with a little bread that has been soaked in milk and then drained. Mix together the meat and pumpkin, and bind the mixture with 2 beaten eggs, a large tablespoon of fresh light cream, and 1 cup of shredded cheese. Stuff the pumpkin shell with this mixture, to not more than an inch from the top, as it swells during cooking. Replace the lid, and wrap the pumpkin in aluminum foil. Cook in a preheated oven at 375° for about 2 hours. Do not be surprised if it takes as long to cook this small pumpkin as the large pumpkin used in the previous recipe—this is because the stuffing requires a little more time to cook. When the pumpkin is tender, take it out of the oven, and remove the foil. Leave the pumpkin to drain for a while before serving in a deep dish.

WINE: Coteaux de Pierrevert rouge

Pumpkin and Spinach Tian

~

A *tian* is a glazed earthenware dish in which we prepare gratins in the oven. I say "in the oven" now that everyone has one. *Tians* traditionally were cooked at the bakers or, if one lived too far from the village, in the fireplace, covered with a sheet of corrugated iron bearing hot coals. So *tian* is the name of a ceramic dish, but as with *terrine* and *marmite*, it has also become the name of its content. In more contemporary French, we say gratin.

There are *tians* or gratins of almost everything—from vegetables to fish, fruit, and even milk—since this cooking method is so common in a typical Provençal kitchen.

But let us start with a *tian* of pumpkin and spinach. The colors and flavors of these two vegetables complement each other perfectly, and this gratin is a truly exquisite dish.

IN THE KITCHEN : You will need 2 pounds of spinach, thoroughly washed. Discard the stalks and the larger veins and blanch the leaves in lightly salted boiling water for about 3 minutes. Drain well and use the leaves to line a buttered gratin dish. Cover with 2 tablespoons of heavy cream and some freshly ground black pepper.

Meanwhile, cut 2 pounds of pumpkin flesh into cubes. Cook over a low heat in a covered pan with a little olive oil, salt, pepper, and a pinch of sugar, until tender, which will take about 30 minutes. Using a fork, mash the pumpkin together with 1 tablespoon of all-purpose flour and 2 egg yolks. Beat the 2 egg whites until stiff, and carefully fold into the pumpkin mixture. Spoon onto the spinach. Sprinkle with some shredded Gruyère cheese and cook in an oven preheated at 375° for about 15 minutes, or until the cheese has melted and is bubbling. Serve immediately.

Pumpkin and Rice Tian
~

Peel a wedge of pumpkin weighing 3 pounds and cut into cubes. Cook in a large covered skillet over a low heat with 1 tablespoon of olive oil, a drop of water, some salt, freshly ground pepper, and a pinch of sugar, until the pumpkin is very tender. Stir with a wooden spoon from time to time. In the meantime, boil ⅔ cup of Camargue round rice (short-grain rice)

in lightly salted water for about 15 minutes. Mix the well-drained rice with the mashed pumpkin, and place in an oven-proof dish. Sprinkle with some shredded Gruyère cheese, breadcrumbs, and a few drops of olive oil. Cook in an oven preheated at 375° for a good 15 minutes, or until the cheese has melted. Leave to cool slightly before serving.

Large and Small Stuffed Cabbages

~

Choose a large round cabbage, firm and tight, weighing at least 2 pounds. Discard the outer leaves. Separate and wash all of the remaining leaves, keeping aside the small leaves of the heart, and blanch for a couple of minutes in boiling water. Drain, immediately refresh in cold water, and spread the leaves out on a towel on the kitchen table.

To make the stuffing: chop, not too finely, the small leaves of the cabbage heart, 7 ounces of ground veal, 7 ounces of pork tenderloin, 3 ounces of bulk pork sausage (sausagemeat), 1 onion, and 3 garlic cloves. Mix well, and add a scant ½ cup of shredded cheese, 2 eggs, ⅔ cup of Camargue round rice (short-grain rice), salt, and pepper. The rice should be uncooked, of course, as its role is to absorb the excess liquid during cooking.

From here on there are two methods, both of which give equally savory results. The traditional method is for a large stuffed cabbage.

Spread a large square of fine cheesecloth on a table. Place the biggest cabbage leaves on top, and spread each with a layer of the stuffing. Continue to alternate layers of leaves and stuffing until, little by little, you have re-created the shape of the cabbage.

Wrap the cabbage in the cloth, and tie tightly at the top. In a pot, not much larger than the size of the cabbage, place 2 carrots, 1 onion, 2 garlic cloves, a sprig of thyme, a bay leaf, and a pinch of salt. Place the cabbage on top and fill the pot with cold water. Cover the pot and bring to a boil. Reduce to a simmer and cook for at least 3 hours. Remove the cabbage from the pot, discard the cloth, and serve whole with some of the broth.

The second method is for small cabbages, which around here we affectionately call *paquetouns*. To begin with, make a thin broth by cooking 2 carrots, 1 onion, 2 garlic cloves, a sprig of thyme, a bay leaf, salt, and pepper in a pot of water until the vegetables are soft and the broth is well flavored. Choose the 10 best leaves of the cabbage. Pile the remaining less attractive leaves onto the 10 best leaves. Place a scoop of stuffing on each pile of leaves, and roll up to form small parcels. Place in a buttered baking dish and crown each parcel with a slice of bacon. Cover with the broth, and cook in a preheated oven at 350° for at least 2 hours, adding more broth from time to time as required.

WINE: Côtes du Ventoux rouge

Field Rabbit with
Mustard Sauce

~

WINE:
Gigondas
rouge

This recipe requires a large rabbit cut into pieces, the same number of strips of bacon as there are pieces of rabbit, a good Dijon mustard, and a lot of thyme. Begin by layering the rabbit in an ovenproof earthenware dish with the thyme, 1 bay leaf, 4 crushed garlic cloves, a little rosemary (too much will overwhelm the other flavors), and 1 sliced onion. Baste generously with olive oil and cook slowly for several hours. Discard the herbs and onion. Brush the rabbit pieces with the mustard, crown each with a generous sprig of thyme and wrap in a piece of bacon.

Arrange the pieces in an oiled gratin dish, sprinkle a few breadcrumbs over each piece, and cook in a preheated oven at 375° for 30 minutes.

Deglaze the gratin dish with some white wine and 1 teaspoon of wine vinegar, and serve the rabbit, very hot, with baked potatoes and a green salad garnished with garlic croûtons.

Garlic Rabbit

~

WINE:
Côtes
du Luberon
rouge

This recipe requires a flameproof cooking pot with a lid—the lid must have a small hole in the top to let steam escape. Cut a large rabbit into pieces and brown in olive oil directly in the pot. When the rabbit is golden, add about 30 unpeeled garlic cloves, a handful of chopped parsley, the juice of 1 large lemon, a pinch of salt, and some freshly ground pepper. Cover the pot and seal the lid with a ribbon of dough made from flour and water. Cook in an oven preheated at 325° for 2½ hours. Serve piping hot, with potatoes with bacon (see recipe on page 26) and a green salad.

*Field Rabbit
with Mustard
Sauce*

Baked
Potatoes
~

Before sharing with you some of my favorite potato recipes, I must tell you about the magnificent potatoes from Pertuis. They are as renowned here as Cavaillon melons, Carpentras strawberries, and Villelaure artichokes. These potatoes grow in the sandy soil of the Pertuis plains on the banks of the Durance. They are exquisite, best cooked in the oven or pot when new, or otherwise prepared as a purée or gratin.

In the kitchen : Peel, wash, and dry 3 pounds of good-size Pertuis potatoes. Cut them into egg-sized pieces. Arrange in a greased baking dish and add 5 tablespoons of water, some chopped thyme, and a pinch of salt. That's all. Cook them in a medium oven for 45 minutes. They should turn golden, slightly larger, and perfectly soft inside. Serve hot with a dab of butter or a sprinkling of good, fruity olive oil.

Potatoes with
Bacon
~

Peel, wash, and dry some medium-size Pertuis potatoes: allow 2 per guest. Cut them into halves, and place a thin slice of bacon across the center. Tie the halves together with some kitchen twine.

Cook over a low heat for 1 hour in a tightly closed pot with a small quantity of neutral cooking oil (peanut, for example). In principle, you should not need to add salt because of the bacon.

Oraison Gratin

~

Oraison is a beautiful village in Haute-Provence, located on the banks of the Durance between Valensole and Forcalquier. There I have eaten a gratin of potatoes, onion, and pork, just perfect after a day's hunting in the woods of Saint-Martin. In the past, it would have been taken to be cooked in the baker's oven, after the bread had been baked. But it will certainly be as good when slowly cooked in your own oven.

IN THE KITCHEN : Begin by making a flavorful broth by cooking 2 leeks, 1 onion, 1 carrot, 2 garlic cloves, a sprig of thyme, a bay leaf, and some salt and pepper in 2 quarts of water. Place a skillet over a low heat and brown 2 large onions, sliced, in a mixture of butter and olive oil. Wash, peel, and dry 2 pounds of old Pertuis potatoes. Slice them finely. In a buttered baking dish, arrange alternate layers of potato slices, browned onions, and shredded Gruyère cheese, beginning and ending with the potato. Add enough of the broth to cover and cook in an oven preheated at 375° for 30 minutes.

For each guest, take a pork cutlet and coat it in a mixture of pepper, salt, and crushed sage leaves. Cover the gratin with the cutlets. Reduce the oven temperature slightly, and continue to cook (approximately 45 minutes) until the cutlets are golden brown.

WINE : Côtes de Provence rouge

Auntie Lilette's Quince Paste

~

Quinces ripen in October, and this is the time to stock up on quince paste. During my childhood, a piece of quince paste on a slice of fresh bread was our 4 o'clock *goûter* (afternoon snack) for a good part of the year. Alas, despite the significant quantity made each year by Auntie Lilette, we always managed to run out. For a few days in October, this golden and fragrant paste was set out to dry in all the available dishes, *tians*, and salad bowls in the house. They were everywhere—all over the kitchen and the pantry.

Once dried, the paste was wrapped in aluminum foil and stacked on the top shelves of the pantry. But the day inevitably came in February when a chocolate bar replaced the fruit paste, and then we had to wait until the following year before enjoying this delicious quince paste once more.

IN THE KITCHEN : Carefully wash 10 or more quinces. Place them in a pot, cover with water, and cook for about 1 hour, or until a knife can be inserted easily. Let cool, then peel and cut into pieces before mashing in a *moulin à légumes* (vegetable mill). Weigh the resulting pulp, return to the pot and add an equal quantity of sugar. Cook for approximately 30 minutes, stirring constantly with a wooden spoon, to dry and thicken the paste. Be careful not to let the paste stick to the bottom of the pot. Then spoon into dishes and spread to a depth of 1 inch. Cover with a towel and leave to dry for 10 days. Turn the paste over and leave to dry once more. When ready, wrap in aluminum foil, which will let you keep it for a long time.

To serve the quince paste, cut it into 1 inch squares, and roll these in sugar.

Pear Cake
~

WINE :
Vin cuit
de Salen,
Domaine
des Bastides

In a mixing bowl mix 2 sticks (8 ounces) of softened butter with 1 cup of sugar. Then beat in 4 large eggs, one at a time, 1 tablespoon of pear liqueur, and vanilla extract to taste. Add 4 cups of all-purpose flour, 2 teaspoons of baking powder, and a pinch of salt. Thin the mixture with a little milk if necessary—but it must remain firm enough to support the weight of the fruit. Pour into a buttered deep cake pan. Peel 6 large pears and cut into quarters. Completely cover the cake mixture with the pear pieces and cook in a preheated oven at 350° for about 50 minutes. You can also make this cake with apples, cherries, blackberries, or plums. Whichever fruit you choose, the recipe calls for about 1 inch of fruit on top.

*Pear Cake
on the
dresser*

Persimmons with rum

~

This is not really a recipe, but for me it's the best way to eat *kakis*—the fruit of the persimmon tree. For a long time I thought that these beautiful Chinese orange-colored fruits, which suddenly appeared in the fall as the persimmon tree lost its leaves, were intended to be used as missiles during epic battles after school. Their extremely bitter taste had completely discouraged me from eating them. But I did not know then what I have since learned—that they lose their bitterness with the first frost. They should not be picked before then. If one follows this rule and waits until they become very soft and almost translucent, they make a wonderful dessert, cut in half, generously bathed in dark rum and sprinkled with sugar.

Persimmon trees

Candied Orange and Lemon Peel

~

This recipe is traditionally made with oranges, but you can also make it with lemons and grapefruit. However, I do advise you to preserve each fruit separately. Choose umblemished and unwaxed fruits with thin skins, wash them, cut them in half, and place in a saucepan with plenty of water. Bring to a boil, lower the heat and simmer for at least 2 hours. The skins should become almost translucent. Drain well, and let cool. Carefully remove and discard the pulp and seeds, and cut the skins into the longest possible strips, approximately ½ inch wide.

At this stage we must pause so that I can tell you how to make a thread syrup. Put 2 pounds of sugar cubes into a saucepan, add 2 tablespoons of glucose or light corn syrup, and 1 cup of water. Place the pan over a low heat until the sugar dissolves, and then gradually increase the heat. Syrup goes through several stages: thread, 230°; soft ball, 234°; firm ball, 244°; hard ball, 250°; soft crack, 270°; hard crack, 300°, and finally reaching caramelized sugar, 310–338°. We are interested in the first stage—a thread syrup. Once the sugar has dissolved, the syrup is brought to a rolling boil; it starts to thicken and is ready when a drop of it drawn between the thumb and forefinger forms a thread. Now add the fruit strips and cook over a low heat for 1 hour. Drain carefully and leave the candied peel to dry on a cake rack. The following day, roll the peel in sugar. Store in an airtight jar.

My Grandmother's Russian Toffee

~

I cherish wonderful memories of a certain tin box, slightly rusty—like the sugar tins you invariably find in the kitchen cupboard—full of thread, buttons, aspirins and Epsom salts, old coins or sugar cubes. My tin had 18th-century dancing *marquises* surrounded by roses on the lid, and it was always filled, as if by a miracle, with small, slightly soft cubes wrapped in silver paper. They were the

best toffees on this earth, my grand-mother's Russian toffees. Why Russian, I have no idea, but that's what she called them, and the name, which sounded so mysterious and exotic, added to the joy of eating them.

IN THE KITCHEN : In a heavy-bottomed pan, place equal quantities of butter, honey, dark chocolate, and sugar. Heat slowly, stirring all the time. When the mixture reaches boiling point, let it bubble for a couple of minutes, until smooth and thick. The less you cook it, the softer the toffee. If you continue to cook the toffee it will be hard—be careful not to let it burn.

Carefully pour the contents of the pan onto a buttered baking sheet—a marble slab would be ideal—and let it cool slightly before cutting into squares. I can-not manage to cut out squares as well as my grandmother. My toffees might not look like much but they taste delicious. Wrap each toffee in aluminum foil and keep them locked away in a metal tin. You are unlikely to be able to keep them for long . . .

Green
Tomato Jam
~

Wash and dry 4 pounds of green tomatoes, then cut them into pieces. Put them in a large preserving pan with a large unwaxed lemon, finely sliced, and 3 pounds of sugar. Bring the mixture to a boil, stirring constantly with a wooden spoon, then lower the heat and cook gently for 30 minutes. You will have to cook the jam for 30 minutes on three suc-cessive days. The jam is ready when a spoonful of the mixture sets when dropped on a plate. While it is still hot, pour the jam into warm, sterilized jars.

You can serve this jam for a snack, or as a dessert, for example with fresh cheese such as *brousse du Rove*, see page 165.

WINE:
Côtes
du Rhône
Rasteau
moelleux

My
Grandmother's
Russian Toffee

CABBAGE AND ROMANCE

For this chapter, I will be a little indiscreet and tell you how a few years ago I wooed the lady who was shortly afterwards to become my wife. It was our first *tête-à-tête* (intimate dinner) and I decided to make my special cabbage dish. It was November, the days were short and a precocious winter was snapping at our heels. We could not possibly have dinner in the kitchen—too mundane. The dining room was too large, too formal, and too boring! I had to find an area that would be both unusual and charming— a wonderful surprise. For a while, I thought of the attic, so romantic and mysterious, but finally I opted for the round-shaped landing on the first floor, with crimson walls, a floor of terra-cotta tiles, and a green terrazzo baseboard which ran all the way up the spiral

staircase to the attic. I brought up a small round table, to echo the shape of the floor, and two chairs, and I set the china and cutlery on a pale gray linen tablecloth. I decorated the room with cabbages, beautiful round green cabbages, planted in terra-cotta pots. I carefully wrapped my gift with a light-blue satin bow. I lit the candles and put a few bottles of wine on ice . . . and started to prepare *la potée d'amour.*

My special cabbage dish at the Château de l'Ange in Lumières

Potée d'Amour
(A Recipe for Love)

~

WINE:
Côtes
du Rhône
Rasteau
rouge

When preparing any magic potion, you will need a special caldron—a large metal or earthenware pot—deep and mysterious. To prepare such a dish for two is a bit of an amusing paradox, and rather greedy. But it can easily be turned into a superb meal for twelve. All you need is an even larger pot and to increase the quantities: I recommend that you begin by cooking a chicken on its own in the pot for about an hour. You should also add a few smoked sausages. But as I am giving it to you, this recipe makes a delicious and very efficient elixir.

IN THE KITCHEN : In the bottom of the pot, place a few thick slices of country-cured bacon, then the vegetables for the soup (except for the potatoes which are added later): a nice firm head of cabbage that has been blanched for a few minutes in boiling water, 2 carrots, 2 turnips, and 2 onions, plus an additional onion studded with cloves. On top of the vegetables, place the meats: a small pork shank, some country-style pork spareribs, a piece of country-cured bacon, and 2 garlic sausages, pierced with a fork to prevent them from bursting. Then, in the middle of all that, a large eating apple. You will also need 3 pieces of star anise, a bay leaf, some freshly ground pepper, and a little salt (not too much, because of the salted meats). Pour 2 large glasses of a good dry white wine into the pot and add enough water to cover the meats. Put the lid on the pot, bring to a boil, then lower the heat and simmer for 1 hour. Then add 2 potatoes and a smoked ham, center slice. Simmer for another hour. Serve piping hot with dill pickles and mustards, but without the broth.

Pot-au-feu

~

This dish is not really suitable for two—it is an abundant convivial dish ideal for sharing with a large gathering of friends around a sizeable table. In most cuisines around the world, similar versions of this recipe can be found. And, of course, there is a traditional Provençal version in which three different kinds of meat are used: beef, lamb, and pork.

In THE KITCHEN : Buy 2 pounds of beef, a shoulder of lamb (or a few lamb shanks), and as many smoked sausages as there are guests. Don't forget a marrow bone. When I have a lot of guests, I always add a veal shank and a cooked chicken. Place all the meats, except for the sausages and the bone, in a large pot, and cover them with unsalted cold water. Bring the water slowly to a boil and carefully skim several times. Lower the heat to maintain a very slow boil and add a large onion studded with cloves, a few unpeeled garlic cloves, a bouquet garni (made with some parsley, a bay leaf, a sprig of thyme, some chervil, the green of a leek, and a celery stalk), a nice piece of dried melon skin, some coarse sea salt or Kosher salt, and a few peppercorns. I normally add 2 or 3 sugar cubes.

Let the *pot-au-feu* cook gently for at least 3 hours. You can then add the white part of a few leeks tied in a bunch, some carrots, a few turnips, a slice of pumpkin, the marrow bone (tied in a cheesecloth bag so that the marrow does not dissolve into the stock), and finally the sausages, pricked with a fork. Cook for another hour. While the broth is still simmering, skim off all the fat with a flat spoon. Serve the broth in separate bowls. If it looks too pale, you can add 1-2 tablespoons of caramel (see recipe on page 41).

Spread the meats and vegetables in a large, warmed serving dish with some potatoes (cooked separately in their skins), and serve with pickles, mustards, coarse sea salt or Kosher salt, and a bowl of *sauce rouge* and *sauce verte* (see recipes on page 38).

WINE: Côtes du Rhône Villages rouge

Sauce Rouge and Sauce Verte

~

La sauce rouge is a simple tomato coulis with a touch of cayenne pepper (see recipe on page 159).

La sauce verte is my friend Bruno's recipe. First, he chops up a big bunch of flat leaf parsley and a garlic clove. Then, in a skillet over a low heat, he cooks the chopped parsley and garlic with 1 tablespoon of butter and 1 tablespoon of olive oil for a couple of minutes. He adds 1 tablespoon of fresh white breadcrumbs and stirs constantly with a wooden spoon until the breadcrumbs are golden brown. Then Bruno adds a dash of vinegar and a pinch of salt and sugar. When the sauce has cooled, all you have to do is thin it down with a little olive oil and serve.

Catherine's Roast Pork with Sage

~

Not long after we were married, I banished Catherine from the kitchen. She didn't mind at all, and all her friends seemed to be extremely envious. However, I would like to point out that Catherine is a wonderful cook, as you will discover from this recipe for roast pork cooked with garlic and sage, on a bed of potatoes *à la boulangère*. Choose a large loin of pork, because it tends to shrink a little when cooked. Anyway, cold roast pork is always delicious.

Put the loin in the center of a large earthenware dish. Peel some cloves of garlic, cut them in half, or quarter them if they are too large, make several deep incisions in the meat, and insert a piece of garlic into each incision. Baste the meat with a little peanut oil, and rub with some fresh sage leaves, and some sprigs of thyme. Season generously with salt and freshly ground pepper. Add a few dabs of butter and a couple of bay leaves, and place the dish in a medium to low oven; the roast should be cooked slowly—about 2 hours for a 3-pound loin. If the meat starts to brown too much, add a few drops of water to the dish and lower the heat, but if the oven temperature is low enough you should not have to do that.

An hour before the roast is cooked, place some peeled potatoes around the meat. Put the roast back into the oven.

Turn the meat two or three times during cooking, at the same time turning the potatoes, to ensure they brown evenly. When ready, the potatoes should be crisp on the outside and tender inside.

WINE: Côtes de Provence rouge

Small Salads
~

After a *pot-au-feu* or a filling dish of cabbage and meat, you can't eat much more than a salad—like this delicious and refreshing salad of carrots, baby zucchini, and spinach. Choose young fresh vegetables. Remove and discard the stalks from the spinach, and wash and dry the leaves. Peel the carrots and the zucchini, and using a vegetable peeler, cut them lengthwise into fine strips. Mix these strips with the spinach and dress them with a simple vinaigrette made with olive oil, salt, pepper, and lemon juice.

Alternatively, serve a nice Banon goats' cheese preserved in olive oil (see recipe on page 40) on a bed of field salad, scattered with a few crushed hazelnuts, or just a simple plain green salad (see recipe on page 96), dressed with an olive oil vinaigrette.

A Jar of
Goats' Cheese
in Olive Oil

~

WINE:
Côtes
du Luberon
blanc

If you go to Banon, do not forget to buy a supply of their famous little goats' cheeses. Buy them fairly dry, so you will be able to preserve them easily in olive oil. Choose a large sterilized glass jar with a lid. At the base, put a layer of these little cheeses and ideally sprinkle them with savory, a herb we call *pèbre d'âse* around here. Savory will flavor the oil and the cheeses, and it will be unnecessary to add any other herbs. You are not making a *bouillabaisse*! Fill the jar with alternate layers of cheeses and savory. Cover with a good olive oil, seal the jar, and marinate for a month before using.

Savory grows wild in southern Europe and tastes like a cross between mint and thyme—thyme could be used instead.

My Cousin Jeanne's
Saint-Honoré

~

Saint-Honoré is a marvelous cake made up of puffs of choux paste, filled with pastry cream, stuck together with caramel on a pastry base, and covered with chantilly cream. Caramel, which gives its deep color to meat stock, its delicate flavor to creams, and its brittle texture to many desserts, is easy to make, if a little tricky. In fact, caramel is the stage sugar reaches just before burning.

IN THE KITCHEN : You will need a saucepan, about 20 sugar cubes and a few drops of water—about 1 tablespoon. Place the saucepan, containing the sugar and water, over a medium heat. First the sugar will dissolve, then start foaming. At that point you will need to concentrate— watch your pan carefully—everything is going to happen very quickly. Suddenly, at the heart of the boiling syrup, there will be a brown spot which will spread rapidly and become darker, smoking a little. Immediately remove the saucepan from the heat and shake it gently to produce an even-colored brown syrup. This is a crucial moment—if you wait just a few seconds longer, the syrup will burn! But if you stop the heat on time, it will take on a lovely color. Too light, it will be tasteless, too dark, it will be bitter. Use it right away while it is still liquid because it hardens very quickly as it cools down. If you want to flavor a custard or color a broth you can also dilute the caramel with a drop of water, which will soften it, but this would be entirely useless for our *Saint-Honoré.*

Let us go back to the beginning of the recipe for the *Saint-Honoré.* To make the dough, in a bowl rub 1 stick (4 ounces) of butter into 2 cups of all-purpose flour, add a pinch of salt, and mix with 1 egg and 1-2 tablespoons of water to form a soft dough. Let the dough rest for 1-2 hours. Roll the dough out to form a ¼ inch thick circle—using a plate to cut out the shape. Carefully transfer the dough to a buttered and floured baking sheet, prick it with a fork, and place it in a medium oven to cook for a good 20 minutes.

Make the choux paste. In a saucepan, bring to a boil 2 cups of water, 1¾ sticks (7 ounces) of butter, 1 tablespoon of salt, and 2 tablespoons of sugar. As soon as the mixture starts boiling, add 3¼ cups of all-purpose flour—all at once. Off the heat, beat the paste with a wooden spoon until it stops sticking to the sides of the pan. Let it cool a little, then add 12 eggs, one at a time, beating well between each addition. Place the choux paste in a pastry bag and pipe small mounds of paste onto buttered baking sheets. Make sure you leave enough space between each mound because they are going to puff up and triple in volume. Cook for about 25 minutes in a moderately hot oven. Any choux puffs not required for the *Saint-Honoré* can be used for profiteroles.

Then make the pastry cream. In a bowl, mix 1 cup of sugar, ⅔ cup of all-purpose flour, 6 egg yolks, and a pinch of salt. Bring 2 cups of milk to a boil and gradually add it to the egg mixture, beating constantly with a whisk until smooth. Pour the contents of the bowl into a saucepan, bring back to a boil, stirring constantly, and cook for a few minutes until the mixture is thick and smooth. Keep stirring the pastry cream until it is cold to avoid a skin forming, which would make it lumpy.

Now make some golden brown caramel. Fill each choux puff with pastry cream and then dip into the caramel. Stick the choux puffs close together around the edge of the pastry and drizzle more caramel over each one. Then carefully pour the remaining pastry cream onto the pastry round, in the middle of the ring of choux puffs. The cake is traditionally decorated with chantilly cream (see recipe on page 196), piped from a pastry bag. The top is decorated with more caramelized choux puffs filled with custard. But for our *tête-à-tête* I chose to cover the cake with a thick layer of chantilly cream, then I placed the cake on a bed of sugar mint leaves; on top I drew a large heart of sugar rose petals, made using the following recipe.

Sugar Flowers

~

Nasturtium flowers, violets, acacia or orange blossom, mint leaves, or rose petals are all perfect for this recipe. Pick the blooms or the leaves from your garden on the same day you will be using them.

For the rose petals, choose unblemished, red, old-fashioned roses, softer and more perfumed than most modern hybrids. Be careful not to bruise the petals.

Beat 2 egg whites until just stiff. Use tweezers to dip the petals and leaves one by one into the egg whites, then into confectioner's sugar. Carefully lay them on a clean baking sheet. Put them in a very low oven, and cook them the same way as you would meringues, but leaving the oven door slightly ajar. The idea is to dry the flowers, not to cook them. Let them cool on a wire rack.

If you are not going to use your sugar flowers or leaves right away, they should be stored in an airtight tin.

My Cousin Jeanne's Saint-Honoré, decorated with sugar flowers

Teatime in the Kitchen

In December, in the clear light of a winter's day, the Luberon becomes a magnificent array of grays, blues, and yellows. If you go for a brisk walk in the afternoon you can work up a warming glow, but as soon as the sun dips down behind the hills, you have to retreat back home.

On your return, having hung the coats and scarves in the hallway, and having run across the freezing corridors of this old barn of a house—too difficult to heat up—you can take refuge in the kitchen, warmed by a bright burning fire and smelling exquisitely of sugar, butter, and vanilla. With rosy cheeks and eyes bright with expectation, everyone is ready for a delicious afternoon tea. On the long wooden table covered with a linen cloth are bowls and cups, a large pot of dark, thick, steamy hot chocolate, a pitcher of warm milk, a slab of sweet butter, some delicious slices of country bread, a selection of cheeses and jams, a splendid fruit cake gleaming with candied fruit or studded with golden raisins, a huge apple and caramel cake and a chocolate cake, together with spice cake smelling of aniseed, and a basket of miniature vanilla crescents...

Chocolate Cake,
Caramel and Apple
Cake and Little
Vanilla Crescents

Pages 46-47:
The kitchen
at the
Château
d'Ansouis

Hot Chocolate

~

It is very simple, but very warming on a cold winter's day. Bring 4 cups of fresh milk to the boil and add 5 squares (5 ounces) of good-quality dark chocolate. Place the pan back over a very low heat and simmer for a few minutes to let the chocolate melt, stirring constantly with a whisk. Serve piping hot.

Fruit Cake

~

The best fruits on this earth are grown in the river valleys of the Rhône and the Durance. They are lined with strawberry and melon fields, cherry trees, peach trees, apricot trees, plum, and pear trees, which are protected from the *mistral* winds by fences and tall cypress trees. So, naturally, not far from those fields and orchards, around Apt and Aix, people have long learned to master the art of crystallizing fruit. In St Rémy-de-Provence, for instance, there is an old factory where the floors are sticky with sugar and the kitchens filled with the vapors of boiling copper pans. The dark, vaulted rooms are piled up with large earthenware vessels overflowing with candied cherries and apricots. In another room, the fruits are carefully encased in lace doilies and placed in little wooden crates before being sent to the four corners of the world. You feel as though you are visiting Snow White and the Seven Dwarfs' jewel mine.

As a matter of fact, it is with these fruit jewels that we decorate the crown for the king on Twelfth Night: angelica for the emeralds, cherries for the rubies.

Fruit Cake and Golden Raisin Cake

IN THE KITCHEN : Let us go back to our *goûter* (afternoon snack). Here is the fruit cake recipe. The day before, soak ⅔ cup of chopped mixed candied fruit (candied peel, melon, peach, and apricot), ⅔ cup of whole candied cherries, and ⅔ cup of golden raisins in as much dark rum as you will need to cover the fruit. The following day beat together 1 stick (4 ounces) of butter with ½ cup of sugar and a pinch of salt until the mixture is smooth and pale. Then, little by little, add 3 eggs, beating well after each addition. Add the grated rind of 1 large unwaxed lemon, followed by 2 cups of all-purpose flour and 1 teaspoon of baking powder. Drain the fruit and add to the cake mixture with 1 tablespoon of the soaking rum (keep the rest in a bottle or a jar—you will be able to use it for your next cake).

Butter a cake mold and line it with nonstick baking parchment. Pour in the batter, allowing enough room for it to almost double in size during cooking. Bake in a preheated oven at 350° for about 45 minutes (the cake is cooked when a skewer, or the blade of a knife, inserted into the center comes out clean). Take the cake out of the oven, invert it on a rack, lift off the mold, and leave the cake to cool. Then wrap it in aluminum foil and wait at least 24 hours before eating. I promise you your patience will be amply rewarded!

Every year, in January, I make a different version of this cake with the leftovers of the 13 Christmas "desserts" (see page 70). Proceed according to the above recipe but replace the candied fruit and the golden raisins with dried figs, tailed and chopped, and pitted dates soaked in rum. You can also add chopped walnuts, almonds, and hazelnuts, pieces of dark nougat, almond paste, and quince paste.

Golden
Raisin Cake
~

Beat 2 sticks (8 ounces) of softened butter with 1 cup of sugar and a pinch of salt until smooth and creamy. Add 4 eggs, one at a time, beating well after each addition, then 4 cups of all-purpose flour and 2 teaspoons of baking powder. Add ½ cup of rum, ⅔ cup of dried currants, and ⅔ cup of golden raisins, and mix well. Add vanilla extract to taste, if liked. Butter a cake mold and line it with nonstick baking parchment. Pour in the cake mixture.

Bake in an oven preheated at 350° for 45 minutes.

Once cooked, invert the cake on a rack, lift off the mold and leave to cool.

Simple Apple Pie

~

First, make the dough by mixing 2 cups of all-purpose flour with ½ cup of sugar, a pinch of salt, and 2 teaspoons of vanilla sugar, if available. Rub in 1¼ sticks (5 ounces) of softened butter until the mixture resembles fine breadcrumbs, and then bind with 1 egg. Lightly knead, then let the dough rest for 30 minutes in a cool place.

In another bowl, beat 1¼ sticks (5 ounces) of butter with ½ cup of sugar, and 1 egg. When the mixture is smooth, gently fold in ¾ cup plus 2 tablespoons of all-purpose flour. Whip 1 cup of heavy cream until it is just stiff, and fold it into the butter mixture.

Roll out the dough and line a pie pan. Peel and core 5 large apples, slice them (not too finely), and arrange them on the dough. Carefully pour the batter over the fruit. Sprinkle with a few slivered almonds and a little sugar. Bake in an oven preheated at 350° for about 1 hour. Let the pie cool down before serving.

WINE: Muscat de Beaumes-de-Venise, served chilled

Caramel and Apple Cake

~

Beat 4 eggs with 1 cup of sugar. (Replace 2 teaspoons of the sugar with vanilla sugar, if available.) Stir in ⅔ cup of melted butter, then gradually add 1¾ cups of all-purpose flour and 2 teaspoons of baking powder.

Make a golden caramel (see recipe on page 41) and pour it into a fairly deep cake pan. Peel, core, and quarter 4 or 5 large apples. Arrange the pieces of apple as close together as possible on the caramel, round side down, and pour the batter over them. Bake in a preheated oven at 350°F for about 30 minutes.

Invert the cake onto a dish as soon as it is cooked and before the caramel has had time to harden.

If you make this cake the day before and wrap it in aluminum foil when it is cold, it will taste even better.

Chocolate Cake

~

Make a syrup with ⅔ cup of sugar and 1 tablespoon of water. When it starts foaming, turn the heat down and stir in 10 squares (10 ounces) of bitter chocolate. Remove the pan from the heat, and stir in 2 sticks (8 ounces) of butter, chopped, 3 eggs (one at a time), and ¾ cup plus 1 tablespoon of sifted all-purpose flour. Pour the cake batter into a large buttered pan. Bake in a bain-marie for no more than an hour in a preheated oven at 350°. Turn the cake out directly onto the serving dish because it should not be handled too much. Once it has cooled completely, cover it with a piece of aluminum foil. The most difficult part is yet to come! You absolutely must hide it in a cool place, but not in the refrigerator, for 24 hours and resist the temptation to serve it immediately.

Another piece of advice: if you have a problem removing the cake from the pan, which happens sometimes, do not worry; just smooth out the surface with the blade of a knife and sprinkle it with confectioners' sugar or powdered cocoa—nobody will be the wiser and the cake will still taste absolutely delicious.

Honey Spice Cake

~

Provence has always produced many kinds of honey—the most famous of all, lavender honey, is far from being my favorite—its strong flavor lacks delicacy. It is such a pity that the great beauty of lavender fields does not transfer itself to the honey! I prefer *garrigue* honey in which the perfumes of lavender, thyme, and all the other flowers of the hills are blended. It is perfect for black nougat (see recipe on page 68), in spice cake or simply spread on a slice of bread. I should also mention acacia honey, which is light and very delicately perfumed.

IN THE KITCHEN : In a large bowl, mix together ½ cup of sugar, 2 cups of all-purpose flour, 1 teaspoon of baking soda, 1 teaspoon apple-pie spice, 2 teaspoons of aniseed, ½ teaspoon of ground cinnamon, and ½ teaspoon of ground cloves. Add 2 teaspoons of rum and 2 tablespoons of honey to 1 cup of boiled milk. Stir with a wooden spoon until the batter is smooth. Cover and let stand overnight at room temperature.

The next day spoon the batter into a greased 1 lb loaf pan lined with nonstick baking parchment on the bottom; the loaf pan should not be more than half full. Cover with foil and bake in a preheated oven at 350°F for 45 minutes. Invert the cake onto a cake rack and let it cool completely before serving.

Orange Cake

~

For this recipe you need: ½ cup of superfine sugar, 1¾ cups of all-purpose flour, 2 teaspoons of baking powder, the grated rind of 1 orange and 1 lemon, the juice of the orange, ⅓ cup of finely chopped candied orange peel, 1 stick (4 ounces) of softened butter, and 3 egg yolks. In a bowl, mix together the sugar, the flour, and the baking powder. Add the grated rinds, the orange juice, and the candied peel, then stir in the butter and the egg yolks. Choose a large shallow pan (for instance a pie or pizza pan) so the cake will not be too deep.

Butter the pan generously and spoon in the cake batter. Cook for 45-55 minutes in a preheated oven at 350°. The cake is delicious eaten when still warm, so serve it right away.

Rose-hip Jam

~

To start with, around October, you will need to find a wild rose bush—you know, the dog rose or the briar type, with plump, bright red fruit, which the dictionary calls *cynorhodons*. You will need a basketful of these. Back home, remove the hips that are too dry; these can be kept for making rose-hip tea when you have a cold—they are very high in vitamin C. With the ripe hips, we are going to make a delicious jam. First, you need to remove the seeds. Split the fruit lengthwise as if you were pitting a date, and scrape out the seeds and any "hairy bits." These "hairy bits" used to be sold as itching powder in joke shops, which is why in Provence, where we call a cat a cat, we have nick-named these "bottom-scratchers."

But let us go back to our jam. Once you have cleaned the rose hips, weigh them and put them in a preserving pan with 3 cups of sugar to each 2 pounds of fruit. Cover and leave to macerate overnight. The following day, cook the fruit and sugar for 30 minutes. You will have to cook the jam for 30 minutes on three successive days. Then pour the jam into sterilized jars.

Serve this jam with large slices of buttered country bread.

Bitter Orange Marmalade

~

We make bitter orange marmalade a little late, in January or February, when the fruit is ripe and when after a trip to the Côte d'Azur, we drive back, the car filled with blooming mimosa to decorate the house, and with baskets of bitter oranges.

In the kitchen : First place 2 pounds of apples, quartered but not peeled or cored, in a pan with 4 cups of water. Cover and slowly cook over a low heat. When the apples are cooked, drain and reserve all the liquid by letting the apples drip from a fine strainer into a bowl.

The copper preserving pan

Meanwhile, pare off the rind of 10 bitter oranges, 10 sweet oranges, and 1 unwaxed lemon. Try to make sure you do not take any pith with the rind. Cut the rind into thin strips and put into a pan of boiling water, then lower the heat and simmer until they are translucent and tender. This will take about 20 minutes. Then drain the rind and discard the liquid.

In a copper pan, mix 1 quart of the apple juice with 2 quarts of orange juice (half bitter orange and half sweet orange juice).

Add the juice of the lemon, the cooked rinds, and 6 pounds of sugar. Bring to a rolling boil and, after a few minutes, turn off the heat and leave the marmalade to cool. It can easily foam and boil over so watch the marmalade constantly while it is boiling. Repeat this operation the following day, and again the day after that. Then you can pour the marmalade into sterilized jars.

Like the rose-hip jam, this marmalade is perfect on buttered bread.

Little Vanilla
Crescents

~

Make a dough by mixing together, with your fingertips, 2 sticks (8 ounces) of butter, 2 cups of all-purpose flour, 1 cup of finely ground almonds, and ⅓ cup of sugar. Let the dough rest in the refrigerator for 1 hour. Then form little moon-shaped cookies the size of a tangerine segment. Arrange them on a buttered baking sheet, leaving room for spreading. Cook in a pre-heated oven at 325°F for about 20 minutes, but watch them constantly because they

must remain pale, and not brown at all. Take them out of the oven and, while still hot, roll them in sugar or a mixture of sugar and vanilla sugar. You must be very careful when doing this because these cookies are fragile and crumble easily when they are still hot from the oven. Let the cookies cool before eating them. I have not mentioned storing them in a tin, because it is virtually impossible to resist eating them all right away.

Bread and butter with rose-hip jam

A CHRISTMAS SUPPER IN PROVENCE

Christmas celebrations start here on 4 December, Saint Barbe's Day. On that day, we go and gather some fresh moss from the hills. We then put the moss in little saucers and sprinkle it with some wheat kernels or lentils and with a few drops of water. During the twenty days to Christmas, the wheat or lentils will sprout into lovely green tufts, symbols of life lying dormant during the winter months, representing the harvest to come. This greenery will find its place among the rocks and the bushes of the Nativity Scene. The most beautiful one will be kept to decorate the Christmas table.

Every year, a few days before the hallowed evening, we go and find the two cardboard boxes put away the year before at the back of the closet, which hold the clay *santons* (ornamental figures for the Nativity Scene) wrapped in cotton wool. The day we set up the Nativity Scene, we leave early in the morning with a large basket, to gather moss to make the fields, sprigs of thyme to represent the olive trees, little twigs of cedar for the pine trees, and some stones of different sizes for the rocks. These can also be made with paper—thick gray paper that is colored with brown, yellow, and red ocher. We used to be able to buy it ready-made at the corner store; we called it crib paper. We also use foil to make the river where we put the fisherman and the washerwoman. A small piece of mirror will do for the pond where the ducks will swim. Back home, we spread all of these on a large piece of cardboard which is placed on the dresser. Then we take the figurines out

The 13 "desserts"

of their boxes and find them a place in this lovely landscape. The Nativity Scene is now ready, but only at midnight will the infant Jesus be placed on his bed of straw between the ox and the donkey. For the people of Provence, Christmas is, of course, a religious feast, but it is also the celebration of the land of Provence, because these little figures in their traditional costumes have, for generations, transplanted the mystery of Bethlehem somewhere between Mount Ventoux and Marseilles harbor.

But let us go back to our Christmas supper, a meal which is both frugal and abundant. The table will be set with three white tablecloths, three candles, and the saucer containing sprouting wheat. There will be no meat. First, the bread, a large loaf marked with a cross, then the *aïgo boulido* (a soup whose name literally means boiled water), celery with anchovies, the *tian* of cardoons, a dish of fresh fish from the coast, eel from the banks of the River Rhône or salt cod from St Malo. Then will come the goats' cheeses served with a curly endive salad "just like baby Jesus' hair" and, of course, the famous 13 "desserts."

I must also mention the log. Not the cake with butter-cream, we will talk about that one tomorrow. I mean the real log, the one celebrated in the ceremony of *cacho-fio*, taken from a dead fruit tree, generally an almond tree. Tonight it is blessed with a little hot wine by the head of the family, then offered to the fire by the youngest member of the family. This ceremony symbolizes the eternity of life. In fact, in Provence, Christmas is the celebration of life—the life of the new-born child, of the wheat germinating and ripening. So mistletoe is not part of the Christmas decor, because it is a cruel parasite, attractive of course, but sooner or later causing the death of the tree on which it grows. Never give mistletoe to a Provençal; he would be a little offended and would decline: "No, my trees are fine, thank you." No mistletoe, and in principle, no Christmas tree either. But as I have previously told you I am half Alsatian, so at home we always had, and we still have, a Christmas tree.

"L'Aïgo Boulido"

~

"Boiled water" is the simplest soup in the world. In Provence, they say *"l'aïgo boulido sauvo la vido"* (boiled water is a life saver), and as a matter of fact, this soup accomplishes miracles after a heavy meal or when you have the flu. Of course, they also add with a touch of irony and a good deal of philosophy, *"au bout d'un tems, tuo li gènt"* (after a while, it kills people), which means you cannot live on boiled water alone. Anyway, it is absolutely delicious and it is the traditional first course of the Christmas supper.

IN THE KITCHEN : You need 3 or 4 garlic cloves per person. Do not peel them, but crush them slightly. Boil the garlic for about 10 minutes in salted water. Then switch off the heat, add a little thyme, a bay leaf, and a lot of sage. Cover the pan and let the herbs infuse. Then strain the soup into a clean pan and heat it again without letting it boil. Serve it with slices of toasted bread moistened with a little olive oil and covered with thin slices of Gruyère cheese which will melt in the hot soup.

Celery with Anchovies

~

At the market, choose a large bunch of white celery. Wash and dry it and discard all the blemished parts. Cut the tender stalks and the white leaves into small pieces.

Take 6 or 7 salted anchovies, wash them under running water and fillet them. Mash the fillets with a fork and put them in a skillet with ½ cup of olive oil, 1 tablespoon of vinegar, and some freshly ground pepper. No garlic is used in this sauce because it would alter the flavor of the anchovies. Cook this mixture over a very low heat—the anchovies must dissolve in the oil without ever boiling. This will take about 15 minutes and you need to stir the mixture constantly. Stir the celery into the warm anchovy sauce and serve immediately from the skillet or in a heated serving dish.

Spinach and Pignoli Pie

~

At this time of year, the greens used are normally either Swiss chard or spinach. Both are delicious, or you can use a combination of the two. Wash the leaves and blanch them in boiling water for 5 minutes. Drain them and squeeze all the liquid out of the leaves.

Make a pie dough with 2 cups of all-purpose flour, a pinch of salt, ½ stick (2 ounces) of butter, 3 tablespoons of olive oil, and 3 tablespoons of water. Roll out the dough and line a pie pan; prick the base with a fork and bake it without any filling in a preheated oven at 350° for 15 minutes. It should not brown at all. Meanwhile, in a bowl, mix 2 egg yolks, ½ cup of heavy cream, 1 cup of shredded Gruyère cheese, a pinch of salt, and freshly ground pepper.

Take the pie shell out of the oven. Arrange the blanched green leaves in the shell then pour the cream mixture over them. Sprinkle with 1 cup of pignoli (pine nuts), decorate with a few ripe olives, and then put the pie back in the oven for a further 20 minutes.

Serve it hot or warm, after the *aïgo boulido*, with the celery and anchovies.

Cardoon Tian

~

Choose a bunch of white cardoons. Wear plastic gloves to peel them, or your hands will be stained for quite a while—that is the one problem with this delicious vegetable. So, peel the stalks and remove all the stringy parts. Cut them into 2 inch pieces. To prevent them darkening, put the cut pieces into a bowl of water to which lemon juice has been added. Meanwhile, add a handful of flour to a large pan filled with water, bring it to a boil, and add the cardoons. Cook for about 1 hour. When the cardoons are nice and tender, drain them. Place the cardoons in a heavy-bottomed pan with 3 tablespoons of olive oil, 1 onion, 2 garlic cloves, coarsely chopped, and 2 anchovy fillets. Cook for a few minutes over a very low heat. Then sprinkle the cardoons with ½ cup of all-purpose flour, mix well and cook, stirring,

Spinach and Pignoli Pie, and Celery with Anchovies

for 1-2 minutes. Pour over 2 cups of hot milk, stirring constantly until the sauce thickens. Season with some salt and freshly ground pepper, and then transfer into a *tian* or baking dish. Cover with some shredded Gruyère cheese and brown in a preheated oven at 375° for 15 minutes. Now, I am going to give you another recipe, not as traditional maybe, but just as delicious, and which does not over-power the delicate flavor of the cardoons. When the cardoons are cooked and very tender, drain them well and put them in a baking dish.

Make a light white sauce with ½ stick (2 ounces) of butter, ½ cup of all-purpose flour and 2 cups of milk. Add salt and freshly ground pepper to taste. When cooked, add a scant ½ cup of light cream and ⅔ cup of shredded Gruyère cheese. Pour the sauce over the cardoons and sprinkle with a little more shredded cheese. Brown in a preheated oven at 375° for 15 minutes.

Truffle Stew

~

I know, you are going to tell me this dish is far too expensive, and too extravagant for Christmas supper—even when you can buy the truffles at the Carpentras market, where they are a lot cheaper than in Paris. But what a wonderful dish! In December, truffles are in full season, and there was a time when, in Vaucluse, truffles were as common as potatoes. They were used in beef stew the way carrots are now. So, on Christmas Eve, after the celery and the cardoon, I always serve this delicious truffle stew.

IN THE KITCHEN : You need at least 2 pounds of truffles. That's right! Brush them carefully, peel them, and reserve the peelings for the creamed salt cod dish we are going to make later on. In a large saucepan, lightly brown a chopped shallot in a little butter and a

WINE: Châteauneuf-du-Pape blanc

Truffles from Carpentras

little olive oil—it should be just golden, no darker. Add half a bottle of white Châteauneuf-du-Pape and cook over a low heat, without covering the pan, until two-thirds of the liquid has evaporated. Season with sea salt or Kosher salt and freshly ground pepper and then add the truffles, cut into ¼ inch thick slices. Stir, then cover and cook for 3 or 4 minutes, only until the stew is hot enough for the truffles to release their fragrance. Serve immediately.

Salt Cod with Leeks

~

WINE:
Côtes
de Provence
rosé

Some people might wonder why cod, caught in the faraway northern seas and salted by fishermen in St Malo, has become so common in Provence that it features in the Christmas supper. It is because the fishermen of St Malo needed huge quantities of salt to preserve their fish, and they found it in abundance on the shores of the Mediterranean and more specifically on the salt flats near the Rhône delta. This is why they exchanged cod for salt. The fish, which kept beautifully despite the hot weather, met with considerable success.

IN THE KITCHEN : The day before, soak 2 pounds of salt cod in water to wash the salt away. Change the water several times during the soaking.
The following day, poach the cod in unsalted water. The water should appear to be trembling; never let it boil. Take 6 pounds of large white leeks. Peel and discard the outer leaves, then wash the leeks carefully. Cut them into 1 inch pieces, and cook in boiling water for 5 minutes. Drain the leeks. In a heavy-bottomed

Cardoons and salt cod

pan put 3 tablespoons of olive oil, a garlic clove, and a small onion, finely chopped. Add the leeks, cover and let them cook over a low heat until very tender. This will take about 20 minutes. Then, add a bowl of ripe olives and the poached salt cod, skinned, boned, and flaked. Mix with the leeks. Add a few tablespoons of the cod cooking water, half-cover the pan and let the mixture simmer for about 1 hour, over a very low heat. Before serving, taste and season with a little freshly ground pepper and a small amount of sea salt or kosher salt, if necessary.

Creamed Salt Cod Tian
~

I ate this for the first time in St Tropez and since then it has always been a part of our family Christmas menu. The day before, soak about 2 pounds of salt cod in a large bowl of water to wash the salt away. Change the water several times during soaking.

Poach the cod in unsalted water, never letting the water boil. Let the fish cool, then remove the skin and bones. Flake it and reserve the nicest pieces—about half of the cod. In a food processor, purée the rest of the fish with a garlic clove, $^2/_3$ cup of olive oil, and the truffle peel if you have made the truffle stew (see page 65). If you are feeling virtuous and are a stickler for tradition, you could cream the mixture using a pestle and mortar.

In another pan, cook 2 pounds of old Pertuis potatoes, peeled, in lightly salted water. When they are cooked, purée them with a masher or in a vegetable mill. Do not use a food processor, or you would end up with potato glue. Add enough hot milk (but not too much) to make a fairly light mixture. Carefully fold in the puréed cod, $^1/_4$ cup of heavy cream, the reserved flakes of cod, and 2 beaten eggs. Season with freshly ground pepper and sea salt or Kosher salt, if necessary. Pour the mixture into a baking dish or a *tian*. Sprinkle some shredded cheese and a few ripe olives over the top. Drizzle a little olive oil over the gratin and brown in a preheated oven at 350° for 30 minutes.

WINE:
Côtes
de Provence
rosé

Orange Fougasse
(Butter Bread)

~

We call it that because it is a *fougasse* recipe from Orange and not because it has anything to do with the fruit of the same name. *Fougasse* is a flat bread from the south of France; it is often flavored with olives or herbs. Everywhere else, it is made with olive oil, but in Orange it is made with butter. At the bakers, buy the equivalent of a baguette of raw bread dough. Knead it with ¾ stick (3 ounces) of softened butter, until the butter has been completely absorbed by the dough. Flatten the dough with your hands and shape it to form an oval about ½ inch thick. Make slits in the dough with a knife, as if you were drawing the veins of a leaf. Then put the *fougasse* on a buttered and floured baking sheet. Make sure you open up the slits. Let it rise for

Christmas breakfast

1 hour, then cook it in a preheated oven at 350° for a good 15 minutes. To serve it you must never cut it with a knife, just break it with your hands, like the bread which was served at the Last Supper.

Black Nougat

~

White nougat is a confection that requires technical expertise, but black nougat can be made easily at home. Buy a sheet of *pain azyme* (rice paper), 2 pounds of set honey, and 1 pound of whole almonds, still in their brown skins.

Melt the honey in a pan, add the almonds and cook for about 40 minutes, stirring constantly with a wooden spoon. The nougat is cooked when a drop of the honey mixture solidifies when it falls into a glass of cold water. Take the pan off the heat and let the mixture cool a bit, still stirring. If the nougat is too hot, it will melt the rice paper. Put half of the rice paper on a marble slab. Make a border with metal rules, like the ones teachers used to punish naughty pupils with. Pour the nougat inside the border on the rice paper, then put the second half of the rice paper on top of it. Take a small bread-board and press slightly on the nougat to make it more compact. Let the black nougat stand for 30 minutes, after which time you can cut it into strips about 2 inches long.

Calissons
~

This marvelous confection from Aix-en-Provence was created a long time ago as a result of a love affair between a pastry chef and his queen. The legend says that the good King René used to go hunting often—too often for his beautiful wife. Queen Jeanne, tired of waiting for him, became very friendly with her young and dashing pastry chef. The young chef, madly in love with his royal mistress, invented a little sweetmeat to please her— the *calisson*.

In Aix-en-Provence, *calissons* are traditionally made with a mixture of almonds and candied melon. In this recipe, I have replaced the melon with orange peel as I prefer it.

IN THE KITCHEN : You need the same weight of almonds and candied orange peel (see recipe on page 31). Blanch the almonds by plunging them in boiling water for a few minutes. Their brown skins will then rub off very easily. Crush the nuts with the candied orange peel using a pestle and mortar or in a food processor if you prefer. You will obtain a grainy paste. Add 2 tablespoons of honey to bind the paste. When it is evenly blended, pour it on a sheet of *pain azyme* (rice paper) on a baking sheet. Spread the paste to form a layer ½ inch thick.

In a bowl, beat 3 egg whites with 2 to 2¼ cups of confectioners' sugar, until you get a smooth and fluid royal icing– this may take 5 or 10 minutes. Spread it over the almond and orange paste. Cut the *calissons* into diamond-shaped pieces and bake them in a preheated oven at 325° for 5 minutes.

The Thirteen "Desserts"

~

WINE:
Muscat
de Beaumes-
de-Venise

Throughout Provence, each family has its own traditional selection of these "desserts," but you need 13 desserts without fail, in memory of Christ and his 12 apostles. I should explain that originally desserts meant nuts and dried fruits, served at the end of a meal. Everyone agrees on the four *mendiants* (beggars): golden raisins representing Dominican monks, almonds to symbolize the bare-footed Carmelites, hazelnuts for the Augustine robes, and dried figs for the Franciscans. Most people also include dates and walnuts, black and white nougat. On the other hand, the choice of fruit varies from one family to another: oranges are sometimes replaced with mandarins, sometimes it is pears or apples, green grapes miraculously preserved in the attic, or a melon suspended since September in a net to keep it from man and beast. In Marseilles, they make *pompe à l'huile d'olive* (olive oil bread), in Aix, a similar bread is called *gibassié*, and in Orange there is the butter *fougasse*. In Vaison-la-Romaine they make apple *panade*, a kind of pie made of bread dough enriched with butter, topped with shredded apple, decorated with a lattice of dough, and flavored with a few drops of orange-flower water when it comes out of the oven, crusty and golden. To all this, you can add quince paste, candied fruit, *calissons*, and sometimes even grapes in eau-de-vie. With these 13 "desserts," we serve *carthagène* (see recipe on page 121) or a muscat wine from Beaumes-de-Venise.

Grapes in
Eau-de-vie

~

To make this alcohol preserve, choose firm grapes. With a pair of scissors, separate each grape from the bunch, leaving a ¼ inch stalk on each one. Wipe the grapes carefully and put them in a sterilized jar. Then fill the jar with a good fruit brandy. Add 2 tablespoons of sugar per quart. Seal the jar, lock it away in a dark cupboard, or secret place, and forget about it for a year.

From Christmas to New Year

The Christmas supper is over and it is time to go to midnight mass. You will eat the leftover *fougasse* tomorrow morning for breakfast, with a large cup of milky coffee. But do not eat too much, because Christmas Day lunch should be full of surprises. It must be a real feast, and for once, we are going to forget the usual simplicity of Provençal cooking. We will buy a plump, white-fleshed chicken from Bresse and a duck foie gras from neighboring Languedoc. At the Carpentras market, we will buy our truffles. Everything else, we have on hand.

Artichoke Salad

~

Choose 12 plump, firm artichoke bottoms. As you clean each one, rub it with lemon juice and then immediately drop it into a bowl of water to prevent it from turning black. Stir 1 tablespoon of all-purpose flour and 2 tablespoons of vinegar (or lemon juice) into 1 quart of cold, salted water in a pan. Bring the water to boil, stirring constantly. Add the artichoke bottoms and cook them in simmering water until just cooked but still a little crunchy. Drain the artichokes and leave them to cool.

In a bowl, prepare a vinaigrette with extra-virgin olive oil, a touch of good quality wine vinegar, and a little sea salt or Kosher salt. Brush and peel 2 or 3 truffles. Reserve the peel to use in the chicken stuffing (see page 72). Cut the truffles into thick slices.

On each plate, make a bed of field salad, and arrange 2 artichoke bottoms on top. Place a slice of pink foie gras and a slice of truffle on each portion. Pour 1 tablespoon of vinaigrette over each artichoke. It is simple but so delicious!

WINE:
Crozes
Hermitage
rouge

Poached Chicken

~

The day before you are going to cook the chicken, you should prepare and stuff it. First, clean the chicken thoroughly. Then prepare the stuffing. Grind 1 pound of veal with the liver of the chicken, 3½ ounces of foie gras, and 1 or 2 truffles. Mix all this with 1 tablespoon of olive oil and 3 tablespoons of cognac. Season with sea salt or Kosher salt and freshly ground pepper. Stuff and truss the chicken. Keep it in the refrigerator until ready to cook.

Place the chicken in a pot, just large enough to hold it. Add 2 carrots, 1 onion studded with cloves, a small bunch of parsley, some sprigs of thyme, a bay leaf, and a leek. Cover with cold water or chicken broth. Add salt and poach, covered, over a very low heat for 1 to 2 hours.

WINE:
Crozes
Hermitage
rouge

Fifteen minutes before serving, melt 1½ tablespoons of butter in a saucepan. Add 1 tablespoon of flour, stir and cook for a few minutes; do not let the flour brown. Take the pan off the heat and gradually add about 1¼ cups of chicken broth. Beat well with a whisk, and return to the heat. Bring to a boil and keep whisking until thickened. Cook for a few minutes longer. Then add ½ cup of fresh heavy cream. Off the heat, mix 2 egg yolks, 1 tablespoon of lemon juice, and a little grated nutmeg in a bowl. Slowly pour the sauce into the egg mixture, stirring constantly. Return to the pan and heat the sauce—but do not allow it to boil. Finish off the sauce by whisking in a small pat of cold butter.

Serve the chicken with Creole rice (boiled rice) and the sauce served separately in a warmed gravyboat.

New Year's Day
Lentils

~

For 1 January, I will give you a recipe for lentils, so that you will be rich all year. In our family (I do not know where the tradition comes from), we say that "if you eat lentils on 1 January, you will have money all year." I think it is a wise, even delicious tradition and so I have always observed it.

*Poached
Chicken*

WINE:
Saint Joseph
rouge

IN THE KITCHEN : Cook 2 cups of chopped onions in a little olive oil over a low heat until they are soft. Add 4 cups of thickly sliced leeks, 4 cups of cubed potatoes, ¾ pound of country-style sausage links, pricked with a fork so they will not burst while cooking, and 2 cups of green or brown lentils, picked over and washed. Cover with cold water—about 3 quarts. Add a dozen unpeeled garlic cloves, some sea salt or Kosher salt, and freshly ground pepper. Cover the pan, bring to a boil, then lower the heat and simmer for at least an hour. Just before serving, add a pat of fresh butter. Drain the lentils and the vegetables, reserving the liquid. First serve the broth in warm soup bowls accompanied by garlic toast and shredded cheese. Then serve the lentils, the vegetables, and the sausages.

"Baïano"
of Chick-peas
~

Here is a meal similar to the dish of New Year's Day lentils. It is a chick-pea soup, eaten traditionally on Palm Sunday when the winter chick-pea reserves were getting low. But before starting the recipe, let me tell you the best way to cook chick-peas. You should cook them in water that has been used for cooking spinach. Then, you do not need to soak them overnight or add baking soda to the cooking water to soften them.

IN THE KITCHEN : If you have not eaten spinach the day before, soak 2 cups of chick-peas overnight in water with a pinch of baking soda. Drain them and rinse them several times. Then place them in a cooking pot with 3 quarts of water, 2 leeks, 1 carrot, a handful of spinach leaves (to facilitate the cooking), 2 garlic cloves, 1 bay leaf, 2 sage leaves, some sea salt or Kosher salt, and freshly ground pepper. When the liquid starts boiling, skim it carefully, then lower the heat, cover the pot and simmer for at least 2 hours, or until the chick-peas are really tender. Add 1 pound of country-style sausage links (pricked with a fork) for the last half hour. When the chick-peas are cooked, take out the sausages and slice them. Drain the chick-peas and keep the broth. Serve it in warm soup bowls with garlic toast and slices of sausage. Sprinkle with shredded cheese. Serve the chick-peas with an *aïoli* (see recipe on page 184) or simply with a good olive oil vinaigrette.

My Mother's
Almond Log

~

Do not be discouraged by the word "log," and try this delicious cake, flavored with coffee and almonds. It must be prepared a day in advance.

First, make a pot of very good, very strong coffee and let it cool.

Put 2 sticks (8 ounces) of butter in a warm place to soften.

Take about 30 almonds, soak them for a few minutes in boiling water and then rub off their skins. Roast the nuts in a hot oven for a few minutes until they are golden. Place them in a strong paper bag and crush them with a rolling pin. Set them aside.

Beat the softened butter with 5 tablespoons of confectioners' sugar. When the mixture is pale and smooth, add 1 egg yolk and some of the cold coffee, little by little, until you have flavored the butter-cream to your taste.

Dip some lady-fingers quickly into the remaining coffee (be careful not to soak them too much). Make the cake by alternating layers of lady-fingers and butter-cream, and forming it into the shape of a log. Keep in mind that you will need about half the butter-cream to cover the outside of the log. Decorate the log with the crushed almonds, to represent the bark of a tree (but not the ends, which are supposed to be the wood). Keep the cake in a cool place, but not in the refrigerator, until the following day.

Under a Winter's Sun

There are winter days, blessed days, when suddenly the *mistral* vanishes, after having blown across the country night and day, taking advantage of every lane, every doorway, every crack in the wood to spread its freezing breath. But all of a sudden, everything stops moving. The sun bursts out through the clouds, flooding the landscape. On these days you must make the best of this gift from heaven.

The stone walls of the Bidaine *pavillon*, still showing traces of their centuries-old ocher color, suddenly take on the most beautiful shade under the light of this pale winter sun. But the light is even more magical inside the yellow sitting room. Opening to the south onto a garden of ornamental ponds; to the east, onto the orchards and the flower garden; and to the north onto a trimmed boxwood walk. Seven high french windows, framed with sulfur-yellow Chinese pelmets, look out onto the gardens. A long couch, a few wing chairs, small tables, and a harpsichord are the only furniture in this living room, which invites you to relax and enjoy life under the impassive gaze of two painted clay mandarins, which seem to have been there for eternity.

What about lunch in this yellow sitting room? Not at a set table but rather a picnic. We will open wide the seven windows of the room, as if it were summer. We will make *oreillettes* (sweet fritters), dry fruit compote, honey spice bread cream, and we will drink muscat wine from Beaumes-de-Venise. We could eat an egg soup or stuffed eggs, and carrot and beef stew. What a wonderful idea! We could even dress up in 18th-century attire, in richly embroidered silk vests, and Ted could play the harpsichord.

And this is how, one February day, we came to have a picnic in the yellow sitting room, dressed up in 18th-century clothes, enjoying the warmth of the winter sun.

Beef Olives

Egg Soup

~

In the old days, every meal started with a soup, and often it was the only plentiful dish of the meal. The one feature common to all these soups was the large slice of bread, sometimes rubbed with a garlic clove, always sprinkled with shredded cheese, that would melt in the hot broth. You find it in fish soup as well as in lentil soup, in cod *bouillabaisse* and in egg soup.

IN THE KITCHEN : The recipe for egg soup begins like the *aïgo boulido* (see page 61) from the Christmas Eve supper. To a pot of salted water add as many as 3 or 4 garlic cloves per person, left unpeeled and crushed slightly. Boil the water for about 10 minutes. Turn off the heat, add a bay leaf, a sprig of thyme, and a few sage leaves, cover the pot and let the flavors infuse. Now you must strain the broth into a clean pan and warm it up again without letting it boil. Then you make a little *aïoli* (see recipe on page 184) and mix it into the broth. Serve with shredded cheese and toasted bread, of course. That is the traditional recipe, but at home, we also made egg soup with any kind of broth: vegetable, chicken, or beef. Try it; it is delicious.

"Brouillade" (Scrambled Eggs)
with Truffles

~

WINE :
Hermitage
blanc

The day before, grate the truffle (or truffles) finely, place it in a bowl and cover it with ½ cup of virgin olive oil. When you want to cook the *brouillade*, beat the eggs, add the truffle and oil, some sea salt or Kosher salt, and freshly ground pepper, and pour into a pan on a double-boiler. Cook for about 20 minutes, stirring constantly. When the eggs reach the consistency of thick cream, take the pan off the heat—it is crucial that the eggs remain creamy and delicate. Add a good tablespoon of heavy cream and keep stirring. Transfer the *brouillade* to a serving dish right away or it will go on cooking. This cooking method is a little tricky but it is well worth it. Serve the *brouillade* nice and hot, with a little field salad.

Stuffed Eggs

~

Allow 2 eggs per person. Hard boil them, peel them, and cut them in half. Spoon out the yolks and place the whites, cut-side up, in a baking dish. In a pan, over a low heat, cook 2 onions, finely sliced, in a mixture of butter and olive oil until they are soft—do not let them color too much. While the onions are cooking, wash and trim 1 pound of spinach. Blanch the leaves in boiling salted water for 3 minutes. Drain, squeezing out as much liquid as you can. Then chop the spinach fairly finely and mix with the onion, the hard-boiled egg yolks, a little milk, and some salt and freshly ground pepper. Fill the egg whites with this stuffing, sprinkle shredded cheese on top, then pour a light white sauce over the eggs. Cook at 375° for 15 minutes.

Spinach and Sardine Tian

~

Wash and trim some spinach leaves. Blanch for 5 minutes in boiling salted water, then drain, squeeze out as much liquid as you can, and chop the leaves roughly. Lightly brown a chopped onion in a little olive oil. Add the spinach and 2 garlic cloves, chopped. Sprinkle with 1 tablespoon of all-purpose flour. Add a little hot milk, some sea salt or Kosher salt, and freshly ground pepper, and mix with a spoon. Pour the spinach mixture into a baking dish. Take 20 good-sized sardines, cut off their heads, remove their insides, and fillet them. Place the fish on top of the spinach, sprinkle over some shredded cheese and breadcrumbs. Drizzle with a little olive oil and brown in a preheated oven at 375° for 15 minutes.

Wine:
Côtes
de Provence
blanc

Potato and Spinach Tian

~

I do not know where this recipe came from—possibly from Nice, or from Alsace, or maybe it was my mother's own creation. Anyway, it was one of my favorite dishes when I was a child, and I give it to you the way my mother gave it to me.

Peel 2 pounds of potatoes and slice them thickly. Place them in a pan of cold water and bring them to a boil, then turn off the heat. Remove the potatoes with a slotted spoon and spread them in a gratin dish. Sprinkle a handful of bacon cubes and 2 onions, finely sliced, over the potatoes. Cover with 2 pounds of blanched spinach leaves (do not forget to squeeze out as much water as possible). Pour boiling milk, seasoned with salt and freshly ground pepper, over the gratin to cover the spinach. Bake in a preheated oven at 350° for about 45 minutes.

Daube from Avignon

~

WINE :
Châteauneuf-
du-Pape
blanc

The traditional pot used to cook this *daube* (stew) is a *daubière*, a large, round, glazed earthenware dish with a lid. The oldest ones appear scorched by days of simmering in the hearth. My clay pot, which I still have today, is shallow enough to fit in my oven. The lid of a *daubière* must have a little hole in it to let the steam escape during cooking. I make a kind of thick ribbon of dough with flour and water to seal the lid to the pot. The cooking is done in a slow oven and all the flavors are trapped in the *daubière*.

This cooking method is perfect for all dishes that need to be simmered. But of course, you can cook them just as successfully on a gas stove if you use a heavy-bottomed pot with a metal flame tamer underneath to diffuse the heat.

IN THE KITCHEN : Bone a leg of lamb and cut the meat into large cubes (the size of an egg). Put the meat into the pot. Add the bone as well, with 1 piece of thick slab bacon, diced. You will also need to add the following ingredients: 2 sliced onions, 2 sliced carrots, a dozen unpeeled garlic cloves, a bay leaf, 3 pieces of dried orange rind, a pinch of freshly grated nutmeg, some salt and freshly ground pepper, and 1 bottle of white Châteauneuf-du-Pape. Leave the lamb to marinate for 6 hours, then simmer in a preheated oven at 300° for 2½ hours, until the meat is very tender. Remove the bone and serve the stew straight from the *daubière*.

Braised Beef with Carrots

~

Have your butcher prepare a nice beef pot roast weighing about 3 pounds, wrapped in beef fat. Dice 1 thick slice of slab bacon and brown in a heavy-bottomed pot with a little olive oil and butter. When the fat is really hot, quickly brown the beef over a high heat, turning it, to seal on all sides. Pour 1 cup of dry white wine over it and let it reduce for a few minutes. Lower the heat and cover the pot with a lid.

After 1 hour, add 6 cups of thickly sliced carrots, 2 sliced onions, and 1 stick of celery and 1 large garlic clove, both chopped finely. If in season, you can add 1 chopped tomato, but never use tomato ketchup. Cover and cook for about another 3 hours. Toward the end, you can add ripe olives or cooked morels, but only at the last minute.

WINE: Lirac rouge

Pages 82-83: The large yellow living room of the Bidaine pavillon

"Brouffade" (Beef Casserole) from
the River Rhône

~

Here is an old recipe for beef with anchovies and capers, well known on the banks of the Rhône, from Arles to Lyon. You will need a large, earthenware cooking pot which will fit in your oven, and a large, shallow baking dish in which to marinate the meat.

The night before, slice 3 pounds of boned beef chuck or bottom round into fairly thin slices. Marinate the beef overnight with 4 tablespoons of olive oil, 2 bay leaves, 6 cloves of garlic, lightly crushed, 2 cloves, and a pinch of freshly grated nutmeg.

The following day, take the meat out of the marinade. Strain the marinade, reserving the oil and the garlic cloves. Finely slice 3 large onions and mix them with the garlic from the marinade. Add 3½ ounces (about ¾ cup) of drained, bottled capers and 12 chopped cornichons.

WINE:
Laudun
blanc

Using a pestle and mortar, mash 6 anchovy fillets with 1 tablespoon of all-purpose flour. Thin the paste with 2 tablespoons of wine vinegar. Transfer the anchovy paste into a large bowl. Stir the reserved oil from the marinade into the anchovy paste, and season with a little salt and plenty of freshly ground pepper. Add the meat and stir to coat.

In the cooking pot, alternate layers of the onion mixture with layers of meat and sauce. Pour 2 cups of water over the meat. Seal the lid of the pot with a ribbon of dough made with flour and water. Bake in the oven at 375° until the *brouffade* is simmering, then reduce the oven temperature to 325° to maintain a slow simmer. The *brouffade* should cook for at least 3 hours, or until the meat is tender. Remove the dough seal and serve immediately from the pot.

Beef Olives

~

For each guest, ask your butcher to cut 3 thin slices of top round of beef, measuring about 2 x 3 inches. On each slice, place a small piece of bacon, and ½ teaspoon of chopped garlic and parsley. Roll the beef slices around the bacon and tie them up with twine. The beef olives are ready.

In a wide, heavy-bottomed pan, heat a little olive oil and add 1 carrot and 1 onion, finely sliced. Place the beef olives on top.

Brown over a medium heat. When the vegetables start sticking a bit, add a glass of dry white wine, then let the wine reduce for a few minutes before adding 2 cups of broth, a bay leaf, a sprig of thyme, a piece of dry orange rind, 2 unpeeled garlic cloves, and the chopped flesh of 2 ripe tomatoes (but never use tomato ketchup). Cover the pan and cook over a low heat for 2 hours.

WINE: Lirac rouge

My Godmother Lilou's
Fennel Compote

~

Julienne (cut into fine strips) a few fennel bulbs and an equal number of onions. In a heavy-bottomed pan, brown the onions lightly in a little olive oil. Then add the fennel, a drop of water, a pinch of salt, some freshly ground pepper,

and 2 tablespoons of mild paprika. Stir well, cover the pan and simmer over a low heat for about 20 minutes, until very soft. Serve hot, with a celeriac purée (see recipe on page 87), to accompany roast beef or lamb.

Endive Compote

~

Do not wash the endive (chicory) heads but wipe them carefully. Discard the inner core at the root end and slice them thinly. In a large skillet over a low heat, cook the endive in butter until all their liquid has evaporated and they are starting to dry out. Add some sea salt or Kosher salt and freshly ground pepper with 1 tablespoon of sugar, and let them brown. Cover the pan and let them soften completely over a low heat for about 20 minutes. Just before serving, add a squeeze of lemon juice and 2 tablespoons of fresh light cream.

This compote is a perfect accompaniment to roast veal or broiled fish.

Mashed Potatoes
with Leeks

~

Carefully wash 1 pound of the white part of leeks and cut them into ½ inch slices. Cook them in boiling salted water for about 20 minutes. Wash and peel 2 pounds of potatoes and cook them in salted water until they are tender. Drain and mash them, or purée them in a vegetable mill. Gradually add a little hot milk until the mashed potatoes are smooth, but not too runny. You are not making a soup!

Add the drained leeks, 1 tablespoon of butter, some freshly ground pepper, and a pinch of freshly grated nutmeg. Taste and add some sea salt or Kosher salt, if necessary.

Mashed potatoes with leeks make a tasty accompaniment for roast chicken.

Celeriac Purée

~

Wash and peel 1½ pounds of potatoes and 1½ pounds of celeriac; cut both vegetables into large pieces.
Boil the potatoes and celeriac together in salted water until they are soft, then drain and mash them. Add just enough hot milk and cream to make a smooth, light purée. Season with freshly ground pepper and sea salt or Kosher salt, if necessary. Serve with red meat or game.

Rosette's Rice Pudding

~

This is a very easy pudding to make. You need 1 quart of fresh whole milk, 5 tablespoons of Camargue round rice (short-grain rice), 16 sugar cubes, 1 vanilla bean, and 1 teaspoon of butter. Place all these ingredients together in a pan and slowly bring to a boil, stirring frequently with a wooden spoon. Pour the mixture into a baking dish and bake for 2 hours in a preheated oven at 325°.
The secret of this dish is slow cooking. The top of the rice pudding should brown lightly, and the underneath should remain creamy, almost like the delicious "milk jam" they make in Argentina.

Edith's Orange and Caramel Salad

~

My friend Edith is a wonderful embroiderer, but she is also an exceptional cook. When she makes an orange salad, she cannot resist embroidering the top with a thread of caramel. It is gorgeous and delicious!

IN THE KITCHEN : Peel 7 large oranges, taking care to remove all the pith

with the skin. Discard the skin and slice the flesh, not too thinly. Place the oranges in a shallow serving dish. Make a caramel with 25 sugar cubes and a drop of water (see recipe on page 41). When the caramel is golden, remove from the heat and add a drop of cold water to stop the caramel from cooking further. Wait a few seconds for it to thicken slightly, moving the saucepan constantly, but do not wait too long or it will harden completely. So, as soon as it has thickened, pour this caramel over the oranges from fairly high up—the way they serve mint tea in Morocco. That way, the caramel will cool and harden slightly on the way down. With a little practice, you will soon learn how to make a nice design on the oranges. Serve the salad fairly soon after adding the caramel, because if you wait too long, the juice of the fruit will dissolve the caramel.

Madame Pavan's "Oreillettes"

~

Theresa Pavan is Italian. She used to be the cook and is still a friend of the Duchess of Sabran-Pontèves in the Château d'Ansouis. Among her many marvelous talents, Theresa made *oreillettes* (sweet fritters) like nobody else, and since she knew I loved them, every year, on Shrove Tuesday, she sent me a basketful. Here is her recipe.

IN THE KITCHEN : Make a dough with 4 cups of all-purpose flour, ⅔ cup of sugar, a pinch of salt, 1 tablespoon of orange-flower water, 1 teaspoon of soft butter, 4 egg yolks, and ⅔ cup of milk. Do not work the dough too much. Form it into a ball and let it rest in a cool place for 2 hours.

If you own a pasta machine, roll out the dough as for lasagne. If not, use a rolling pin and roll out a sheet of dough about ¹⁄₁₀ inch thick. Cut out strips measuring 6 x 3 inches and make a slit in the center of each strip. Deep-fry the fritters in hot peanut oil, take them out as soon as they are golden and let them drain on paper towels. Sprinkle them with confectioners' sugar or sugar. In the old days, they would have been fried in olive oil in a skillet. I have tried them this way and they are delicious, but the flavor is a little strong.

Véronique L.'s
Dried Fruit Compote

~

WINE:
Côtes
du Rhône
Rasteau
moelleux

Heavenly Véronique, who looks as if she has just stepped out from a Watteau painting, is swirling in her dress, laughing, and leaning over to one side while she lightly dips a dried apricot into honey spice cake cream.

IN THE KITCHEN : Put 2 cups of pitted prunes, 2 cups of pitted dates, and 2 cups of dried apricots in a saucepan.

Cover them with 1 cup of tea, the juice and the grated rind of 2 large oranges, a generous pinch of ground cinnamon, and 4 tablespoons of clear honey. Cover and cook over a low heat for 15 minutes. Take the pan off the heat and add 2½ cups of pignoli (pine nuts). Pour into a pretty compote dish and leave for a few hours before serving with honey ice cream or spice cake cream.

Véronique L.'s
Spice Cake Cream

~

Wash ⅓ cup of golden raisins and let them soak in boiling water for 10 minutes. In a saucepan, bring 1 cup of milk to a boil, together with 1¾ cups of light cream and a vanilla bean, split in two. Let the vanilla bean infuse in the liquid for 10 minutes. In a large bowl, mix 1 tablespoon of honey with 2 egg yolks and 1 teaspoon of aniseed. Gradually pour the hot milk and cream onto the eggs.

Return to a clean pan and cook for a few minutes over a low heat until the cream thickens, stirring all the time. In a deep dish, crumble ¾ pound of very good spice cake, pour the boiling hot cream over it and beat with a whisk until the mixture is smooth. Add the drained golden raisins. Let the cream cool, then chill in the refrigerator for about 3 hours before serving.

*Dried Fruit
Compote and
Spice Cake
Cream*

A Spring Lunch

For a long time lamb has been an indispensable part of Easter lunch. When people had huge fireplaces, they used to roast a whole lamb—the "Pascal lamb." Now, most of us make do with just a leg. But the fact remains that the best way to cook this roast is on a spit over a log fire. You need some nice oak logs, and in front of the fire an antique spit, which will turn the meat slowly before the flames. They are extremely simple but most of them still work beautifully. So skewer your leg of lamb on the spit, without studding it with garlic cloves or anchovies, because the slits would allow the meat juices to escape. For the same reason, season it with salt only toward the end of the cooking time. Just before salting the lamb, "flame" it. I will tell you how to "flame" it by sharing another nice story: the tale of the *brochette* of thrush.

It happened one winter, in a beautiful fireplace in Vinsobres, at the boundary between the Drôme and the Vaucluse. The men had killed the birds and the women had prepared them. The men kindled the fire, and they skewered the birds, belly up, heads pointing toward the outside of the spit, because as Jeannot explained, "when they turn, they drip and when they drip, the juices run along the beaks and drip onto the bread." The "bread" consisted of large slices of bread, placed immediately under the roast on a dripping pan. So, they placed the birds on the spit, heads out, interspersed here and there with a nice piece of pork belly because, Jeannot went on, "there are always those who are not keen on thrush, so there is no waste." The birds were seasoned with a little

Back from the market

salt and freshly ground pepper, and all that remained was to cook them above a steady fire for about 3 hours—not forgetting to move the slices of bread around from time to time. They were all looking at the spit turning slowly, waiting for the moment to "flame" the birds. To do that, they had a kind of metal funnel on which a handle had been soldered. The funnel was placed in the fire to heat it up. When it was red hot and the birds were almost cooked, a piece of bacon fat was placed inside the funnel. The bacon melted instantly into a kind of rain of fat that showered all over the birds. The birds were then served on the bread and, believe me, soon only "the beak and the tail" were left.

WINE:
Vinsobres
rouge
or Côte
Rôtie

But this is spring, the table is set in the garden, and besides the leg of lamb, I have prepared a nice green salad, some asparagus from Lauris with a "simple" little sauce, a dish of morels and sausages, all the lovely spring vegetables from the garden, a superb strawberry cake, and some unusual acacia fritters.

Lauris Asparagus
with Truffles

~

As for the scrambled eggs (see recipe on page 78), you will have to grate the truffles finely the day before and let them marinate in ½ cup of virgin olive oil overnight.

The following day, just before serving, you just need to add a little salt and pepper, and a dash of vinegar. And there you have the perfect sauce to go with the beautiful asparagus from Lauris.

Choose thick white asparagus with green and purple tips. Carefully wash and peel the asparagus stalks (do not touch the fragile tips) and cook them in boiling salted water for about 15 minutes—they will need a little longer if they are really big. But be careful, asparagus should not be

overcooked; they should still be a little crisp to the bite. Drain well and serve warm with the truffle vinaigrette.

Wild Asparagus
Omelet

~

In Provence in the spring you can find wild asparagus under bushes and in the vineyards. They grow into long, curved, slim stems, and you should use only about the first 8 inches from the tip.

Blanch the asparagus for 10 minutes in boiling salted water, and then drain. With a fork, scrape away the hard parts at the bottom of the stems and cut the remaining asparagus into 4 inch lengths. Put a little olive oil in a skillet, and lightly brown the asparagus over a medium heat for 5 minutes. Add the beaten eggs, salt, and freshly ground pepper, and sprinkle with some shredded Dutch cheese.

Let the eggs cook for a few minutes on one side, then flip the omelet over and cook it on the other side.

To flip the omelet over, you can slide it onto a traditional Provençal *vire-omelette* ("omelet flipper") which is an invaluable disk of glazed clay (see illustration on page 140). If you do not have one, a pan lid will do just as well.

Green Salad
~

It was traditional in Provence to start lunch with a green salad, which was always dressed with an olive oil vinaigrette made according to the "4 people" rule: a miser for the vinegar, a wise man for the salt and pepper, a rich man for the oil, and a madman to mix it.

In the kitchen : With field salad, called *doucette* in Provence, add to the basic "4 people" vinaigrette 2 finely sliced onions which have been softened slowly in olive oil.

With chicory, use the same vinaigrette and serve with garlic croûtons, which should be added just before mixing the salad or they will become soggy. You can also add a few sliced ribs of celery.

With dandelion leaves or wild herbs (which in Provence can be picked in the country or bought at the market), flavor the vinaigrette with 2 or 3 anchovy fillets and 1 garlic clove, both finely crushed.

With romaine or bibb lettuce, finely chop a few scallions or olives and add with sliced hard-boiled eggs.

Finally, with arugula, add some shavings of very dry Banon goats' cheese and use lemon juice instead of vinegar. Shavings of Parmesan cheese are delicious, too.

Romaine lettuce and bibb lettuce

Pages 98-99: Jacques Grange's Mas Mireo

Salad of Purple
Artichokes from Villelaure

~

This is another spring salad which is slightly bitter but very delicate in flavor. Clean some baby purple artichokes from Villelaure and slice them finely. Pour some lemon juice over right away, mix well and add some olive oil, salt, and freshly ground pepper. That is all, and it is really, really good!

Artichoke
Omelet

~

Select some small purple artichokes, remove and discard the hard outer leaves and the stem. Cut the artichokes in half. Remove the chokes if there are any, but if the artichokes are young, there should not be much. Slice them finely and cook in some olive oil over a low heat until golden. When they are ready, use as the basis for an omelet, following the recipe on page 95 for Wild Asparagus Omelet.

Homemade
Ravioli

~

This ravioli is large and square, made of dough which is filled and then cooked in boiling salted water. It has nothing to do with the tiny ravioli from the town of Romans, which is a delicious version generally served as a first course and which I personally prefer pan-fried until nice and crunchy and served with drinks (see recipe on page 127).

IN THE KITCHEN : Start with the dough: put 4 cups of all-purpose flour on a smooth work surface and make a well in the center. Break 5 eggs into the well. Add a good pinch of salt and 3 tablespoons of olive oil, then mix with your fingers to form a dough. Lightly knead the dough until it is smooth and elastic. Let it rest for an hour.

Meanwhile, we will prepare the filling. I am going to give you three delicious recipes, all of them using spinach leaves which have been blanched for 5 minutes in boiling salted water, drained, squeezed dry, and then chopped finely.

First, a classic recipe—Meat Ravioli. For this, use ⅔ pound of leftover *daube* or stewed beef. Grind the meat and then mix it with 1¼ cups of finely chopped, blanched spinach. Finely chop 2 onions and brown in olive oil. Add the onions with 3 egg yolks to the meat and spinach filling. Mix together and season to taste.

Another classic recipe—Cheese Ravioli. Mix together 1¼ cups of fresh *brousse* cheese (see page 165) with 1 cup of shredded Gruyère cheese, and 3 egg yolks. Add 1¼ cups of finely chopped, blanched spinach. Mix together and season to taste.

Finally, a more original recipe which personally I like very much—Ravioli with Mussels. Cook 1 ear of corn in boiling salted water, then remove the kernels. Place the kernels in a food processor or blender and liquidize. Scrub and beard 1 quart of mussels. Put them in a covered pot over a high heat with a chopped garlic clove and a dash of olive oil. Cook them for a few minutes until the shells open, discarding any mussels that remain closed. Carefully remove the mussels from their shells and mix them with 1¼ cups of finely chopped, blanched spinach, the creamed corn, and 3 egg yolks. Season to taste.

Now, for the dough, ideally you would use a pasta machine, but you can also use a rolling pin. Roll out the dough on a floured surface into paper-thin sheets. Cut the sheets into 3 inch squares. On half of these squares, put 1 tablespoon of the filling you have chosen, then cover with another square of dough. Seal the ravioli all around with your fingers. Bring a large saucepan of water to a boil, add a handful of salt and 1 tablespoon of oil. Plunge the ravioli into the boiling water. They are ready when they float to the surface. Carefully take them out with a slotted spoon and serve them right away, with a dash of olive oil drizzled over them. A stronger sauce would mask their delicate flavor.

Leg of Lamb with
Garlic Cream Sauce

~

WINE:
Côtes
du Luberon
rouge

Ideally roast your leg of lamb on a spit. Alternatively baste it with a little oil and bake it in a hot oven. Allow 20 minutes cooking time for each pound of lamb. Meanwhile, boil about 10 whole garlic bulbs, still in their skins. After 10 minutes, drain and discard the water, and replace it with fresh boiling water. Cook the garlic for another 10 minutes. Drain the garlic and then peel and mash it.

When the lamb is cooked, sprinkle it with sea salt or Kosher salt, then deglaze the meat juices in the dripping pan, or roasting pan, with a little hot water, scraping up all the brown bits. Add the mashed garlic and stir until well mixed. Serve this creamy garlic sauce in a warmed gravy-boat with the carved lamb.

Roast Kid
with Anchovy

~

WINE:
Côtes
du Luberon
rouge

You will find that good-quality kid meat is available around Easter. Kid meat is best roasted but needs stronger seasoning than lamb.

As when cooking lamb, roast it on a spit or in the oven. Place a few lemon slices around the meat, with 10 or 12 garlic cloves still in their skins, 10 or 12 anchovy fillets, 1 cup of water, and a few cubes of fatty bacon. If you are baking the roast, do it in a hot oven, allowing about 20 minutes per pound. Baste and turn it over several times, and salt toward the end of the cooking time. Add a little water from time to time if necessary. When the roast is ready, transfer it to a warmed serving platter. Remove the garlic cloves, peel them and return them to the roasting pan. Discard the lemon slices. Deglaze the roasting pan with a little boiling water, mashing the garlic and the anchovies into the gravy. Serve with the roast.

A Stew of
Spring Vegetables

~

Have you ever visited the market in l'Isle-sur-la-Sorgue, a large wicker basket on your arm, on a beautiful spring morning? I know I am overly partial to this market, as well as those in Carpentras and Saint-Rémy, and I apologize. In fact, all the markets in Provence are wonderful. In the spring, the River Sorgue is high and clear, the sun shines brightly through the new leaves on the trees, the air is cool and light, and the market stalls are covered with gorgeous greens and new vegetables. They are so appetizing, so tender, so pink, so green that you do not know which to choose: the fava beans or the carrots, the tiny purple artichokes picked from the plant so that more can grow, the translucent snow peas, or the baby onions, white and plump. There's no need to decide between them—buy a little of everything and make a delicious stew of spring vegetables.

IN THE KITCHEN : You will need all these lovely spring vegetables: potatoes, carrots, baby white onions, peas, fava beans, snow peas, small purple artichokes, and lettuce hearts. Wash all the vegetables carefully. Do not peel the potatoes or the artichokes and only scrape the carrots if absolutely necessary. Remove the outer skin of the onions, top and tail the snow peas and the fava beans, and clean the lettuce hearts. Place them all in a heavy-bottomed pan with 3 tablespoons of olive oil, 3 tablespoons of water, a pinch of sugar, some sea salt or Kosher salt, and freshly ground pepper. Cover the pan and let the vegetables cook slowly for 30 minutes.

Morels with Pork Sausages

~

In the spring, in the sandy soil of the Luberon foothills, you can pick basketfuls of *mourigoulo*, morel mushrooms. In l'Isle-sur-la-Sorgue, we eat them with long, thin, fresh pork sausages which we call *saucissettes* and which are delicious broiled.

WINE: Séguret rouge

IN THE KITCHEN : Cut off the sandy stem of each morel. Wash the caps carefully, and dry them well. Cut the larger ones into 2 or 3 pieces.

You will need 2 sausages per person. Prick them with a fork so that they will not burst when cooking. Brown them in a skillet to render some of their fat.

When the sausages are cooked, remove from the skillet and keep them warm. Add a small pat of butter and 1 tablespoon of olive oil to the skillet. When the fat is hot, add the mushrooms. Season with sea salt or Kosher salt and freshly ground pepper. Let the mushrooms cook until all the water has evaporated. Return the sausages to the skillet with the morels and warm them through for 2 minutes. Sprinkle with chopped parsley and serve piping hot.

This recipe can also be made in the fall, using a variety of different mushrooms, some of which benefit from the addition of chopped garlic with the parsley.

Artichokes "en Barigoule"

~

Barigoulo or *berigoulo* is the Provençal word for mushroom. It is also the word used to describe the wide-brimmed felt hats which country women used to wear. This recipe has been given the same name, probably because the prepared artichokes look a little like mushrooms.

IN THE KITCHEN : Use 4 pounds of small, tender, purple artichokes. Discard the tough outer leaves. Using a sharp knife, cut off the tops of the artichokes, then cut the bottoms into halves or quarters, depending on their size. Remove and discard any chokes you find,

Morels with Pork Sausag

but if the artichokes are really small, they will not have chokes, so they can be left whole. As you prepare the artichokes, drop them into a bowl of water acidulated with vinegar or lemon juice so they will not turn black. Use 1 pound of small white onions, whole, or 2 large onions roughly chopped. Wash 2 small lettuces and cut them into strips. Dice 10 bacon slices.

In a heavy-bottomed pan, heat some olive oil and brown the onions and the bacon. Add 10 or 12 unpeeled garlic cloves, the artichoke hearts, the strips of lettuce, some freshly ground pepper, and a little salt (but not too much, because of the bacon). Add ½ cup of water. Cover the pan and simmer for 1 hour. If necessary, add some water from time to time.

The Countess' Potatoes
~

Imagine an aristocrat from the Alpille Hills, barefoot, sleeves rolled up, skirts tied up in her belt. She is busy around the cooking pots, dishing out food with a smile, seemingly without effort. She is our friend Françoise, the Countess.

IN THE KITCHEN : For this marvelous stew, you need approximately equal quantities of potatoes and seasonal vegetables, whatever you have on hand. For instance, artichokes, baby onions and fava beans, or carrots, turnips and the white part of leeks, or eggplant, sweet red peppers and tomatoes. With spring vegetables, of course, the potatoes should be new baby potatoes. Pertuis potatoes are ideal for this recipe. Any large vegetables should be cut into pieces.

Wash and peel the vegetables. Cut them into 1-1½ inch pieces. In a heavy-bottomed pan, heat 2 or 3 tablespoons of olive oil and brown 2 chopped onions. Add 3 unpeeled garlic cloves, 2 bay leaves, a sprig of thyme, the potatoes and the vegetables, 3 tablespoons of water, and salt and freshly ground pepper to taste. Cover and cook over a low heat for at least 30 minutes. Add a little extra water if necessary. About 10 minutes before serving, add a bowl of ripe olives, and lightly stir with the vegetables, to avoid mashing them. Let the olives heat through before serving.

My Strawberry Cake

~

This is the cake I always made every year for Mother's Day. It was a whole morning's work, and it would have been much worse if my mother had not played the role of a young chef's help, washing and drying plates and spoons as I went along.

I do not remember where or when I discovered this recipe, but it is absolutely delicious and rather spectacular.

IN THE KITCHEN : In a bowl, beat 4 eggs with 2 tablespoons of hot (but not boiling) water. Stir in ⅔ cup of sugar, 1 tablespoon of vanilla sugar (or more sugar), then add 1 cup of all-purpose flour, ¾ cup of potato flour, and 1 tablespoon of baking powder. Pour the batter into a buttered, deep cake pan and bake for 30 minutes or until cooked through in a preheated oven at 350°F. Then invert the cake on a wire rack and let it cool.

Whip 2 cups of heavy cream and flavor it with a little vanilla sugar or sugar flavored with vanilla extract. Using a long-bladed knife, cut the cake horizontally into 3 or 4 layers, each about ½ inch thick. Spread raspberry jam over the bottom cake layer, cover with slices of fresh strawberries, then with some whipped cream. Repeat these layers, finishing with the top cake layer. Cover the whole cake with the remaining whipped cream and decorate with whole strawberries.

Auntie Lilette's Strawberry Cake

~

In our family, we have another strawberry cake to rival the first one. It is simpler, lighter, very delicate, and just as delicious—so much so, that we have never been able to agree on which was the best. This is my Aunt Elisabeth's recipe.

IN THE KITCHEN : Crush 1¼ cups of strawberries with a little sugar. Pour this strawberry purée into a plastic tray and place in the freezer. While the sherbet is hardening, weigh 5 eggs in their shells. You require the same weight of sugar and half the weight of potato flour. Separate the eggs. Beat the yolks with the sugar until the mixture is smooth and pale. Beat the egg whites with a pinch of salt until they hold firm peaks. Carefully fold the potato flour into the egg yolks, then very lightly fold in the egg whites.

Pour into a buttered cake pan, and bake in a preheated oven at 350°F for 30 minutes. Then invert the cake on a wire rack and let it cool completely.

Cut it in half horizontally and fill it with the sherbet. Cover the cake completely with whipped cream and decorate with whole strawberries. This cake must be assembled at the last minute.

Acacia Blossom Fritters

~

You will find acacia trees everywhere in Provence, tall, elegant trees which in April are covered with lovely, white blossoms. It is with these that we are going to make our fritters, having taken a basket and gathered some of those beautiful fragrant clusters from the tree.

IN THE KITCHEN : In a bowl, make a batter with 2 cups of all-purpose flour, a pinch of salt, and ⅔ cup of water. Add 1 egg and 1 tablespoon of olive oil. Beat the batter until it is smooth and then let it rest for an hour or two.

Just before making the fritters, beat 2 egg whites with a pinch of salt until stiff and then fold them lightly into the batter.

Heat 1 inch of oil in a skillet. Dip the acacia blossoms in the batter and plunge them into the hot oil. Once golden, turn them over and then take them out with a slotted spoon. Let them drain on a piece of paper towel. Sprinkle with sugar and serve warm.

Acacia Blossom Fritters

Breakfast with the Horsemen

In the Camargue, life starts at daybreak. Just enough time to drink a cup of coffee, and then *les gardians* (horsemen) are on their horses. There is not a morning when they do not have to ride over earth or water to muster or separate the herds of bulls. As for me, well, I am not a good horseman, and by nature more contemplative than active. I prefer to stroll around, and I go and "take the pulse of the lake," watch the birds, and float in and out of day-dreams, in this strange land. So, when around 10 o'clock we go back to the house, a little tired and feeling hungry, what a joy it is for me and *les gardians* to see the table set under the tamarisk trees and smell all the aromas of the meal prepared by the ladies of the house. The dried sausage from Arles and the olives, the salad of cuttle-fish with warm potatoes and aïoli, the broiled eggplant, the jar of *cachat* (cheese), and the rice pudding. Not forgetting the *Carthagène* wine shining golden in the sun.

The horses of the Camargue grazing on a prairie

Watermelon Jam and "Carthagène" wine

Broken Olives

~

Olives and the dried sausages from Arles are inseparable companions. The olive harvest season starts here in September. At that time, the olives are plump but still green. It is with these olives that you will prepare "broken" olives. In October, they turn purple. At the end of November, they are black and full of oil, so you would then be able to prepare "pricked" olives. Olive harvesting for oil-making will go on until Saint Blaise's day, at the beginning of February, as the saying goes: *"Per Santo Catarino, l'oli es à l'oulivo, Per San Blaise, l'es encore mai"* — "on Saint Catherine's day, the oil is in the olive. On Saint Blaise's day, there is even more."

IN THE KITCHEN : The first olives, the green ones, harvested in September, are acid and bitter, and before you can eat them, you will have to get rid of this bitterness. Take 3 pounds of freshly picked green olives, and split them one by one with a wooden mallet, but do not crush them. Soak the olives in cold water for at least a week, changing the water every day. My friend Annie Laurent does this every day for a whole month. On the last day, put ⅔ cup of coarse salt or Kosher salt, 1 sprig of fennel, a few bay leaves, 3 or 4 unpeeled garlic cloves, and a piece of dried orange rind into a large pan with 3 quarts of boiling water. Remove the pan from the heat and let all the flavors infuse in the water until it is completely cold. Drain the olives, place them in a glazed earthenware pot, and cover them with the flavored salted water. Cover the pot and store in a cool place, but wait for a week before eating the olives.

Be careful not to leave them too long though, because they will not keep for more than about 2 months.

Pricked Olives

~

Black olives are less bitter than green ones, especially if you can wait for the olives picked in January, *les grossanes,* fully ripened, full of oil and a little wrinkled. All you need to do then is to prick them several times with a needle. To speed up the process, my grandmother used to make little "pricking brushes" by sticking several pins through slices of cork (cut from a wine cork) and placing us children in charge of this operation. A prick on one side, a prick on the other, and the olive was ready!

After pickling the olives, put them in a shallow dish and cover them with fine salt to remove any moisture.

The following day, rinse them carefully in fresh cold water and place them in a glazed earthenware pot with lots of thyme, a sprig or two of rosemary, a few bay leaves, 3-4 whole garlic cloves, 1-2 small hot chiles, if you like them, and enough olive oil to cover.

This recipe can be made in large quantities, and the olives will keep until next season without any problem.

"Meissounenco à la Sucarello"

~

At most Provençal markets, you can buy snails, and more often than not, the peasant who is selling them will have already made sure they have discharged their slime (by "purging" them, or starving them for a certain time), so you can use them straight away. These snails are of a reasonable size, though they are much smaller than Burgundy snails, and are delicious broiled over hot coals or cooked in boiling water flavored with herbs and served with an *aïoli* (see recipe on page 184). But to make our *sucarello*, we need the tiny snails which come out in the morning dew and which, as soon as the temperature rises, climb up to the top of fennel plants, wooden posts or even trees. They are nicely striped yellow and gray,

and we call them *limaçons* or *meissounenco*. You will not find these at the market. So, pick up a wire basket and go and find about a hundred of these dew snails.

IN THE KITCHEN : These snails are so small it is not necessary to "purge" them to cleanse their insides, but they do need to soak for about 12 hours in a large bowl filled with water to which a cup of salt and a cup of vinegar have been added. At the end of that time, rinse them several times in fresh cold water. For the next step you need a little patience, because the top of the spiral of each shell must be pierced using a sharp kitchen knife. That way, it will be easier to suck the snails out of their shells, once they are cooked. That is how we eat them, *à la sucarello*.

Cook the snails in a well-flavored broth with some fennel, some thyme, a bay leaf, and a piece of dried orange peel. Boil the snails for 30 minutes, then drain them thoroughly.

Prepare a vinaigrette with a little vinegar, olive oil, salt, and freshly ground pepper. Just before serving pour the vinaigrette over the snails, and sprinkle with chopped fresh parsley.

Fisherman's "Rouille" (Potato Salad) from Les Marquises

~

Les Marquises is the name of my friends Henri and Annie Laurent's beautiful property, which lies between Lake Vacares and the man-made salt marshes of Giraud. At Annie's table, we enjoy the generous and genuine food of the Camargue. Often the meal starts with the marvelous fisherman's *rouille*. As a matter of fact, this is a *rouille* in name only. It has nothing to do with the real *rouille*, which is a sauce deriving its name from the color and the flavor of Spanish sweet red peppers and which is used to enhance fish soups and *bouillabaisses* (see recipe on page 130). In this *rouille*, there are no peppers, no orange color, just a small teaspoon of mustard in an *aïoli*, a heresy which might shock traditionalists but which gives, as I have told you, a superb result.

IN THE KITCHEN : This potato salad requires a little organization because it must be served very hot or it will lose all its character. I will give you the proportions for 12 people. First boil 4 pounds of potatoes in their skins in a pan of salted water, with 1 leek, 1 onion, 1 garlic clove, 2 bay leaves, a little thyme, and some white pepper. Then, prepare 4 pounds of cuttlefish. Remove the bones and the ink sacs,

Fisherman's "Rouille"

and cut the fish into 2 inch squares. Prepare a broth with 3 cups of water, 1 cup of dry white wine, 1 leek, 1 onion, some lemon slices, some garlic, some fresh herbs, some sea salt or Kosher salt, and a little freshly ground pepper.

Simmer the broth for 15 minutes, then lower the heat and add the cuttlefish. Continue to cook for about 20 minutes. Meanwhile, prepare an *aïoli* (see recipe on page 184), adding a teaspoon of Dijon mustard to the garlic and egg yolk mixture before incorporating the olive oil. Drain the potatoes, then peel and dice them. Drain the cuttlefish, discarding the broth, herbs, and vegetables. Mix the potatoes and the fish with the *aïoli*. Serve this fisherman's *rouille* right away, while piping hot. I personally present it in a warm soup tureen with a lid.

"Tellines à l'aïoli"
~

A *telline* is a small bivalve shellfish which lives on the sandy beaches of the Camargue. You can find them at all the good fishmongers in Provence. First, soak the *tellines* in fresh water overnight to get rid of their sand. Then you need to prepare a good *aïoli* with 2 cups of oil, using the recipe on page 184. Just before serving, in a large saucepan, bring to a boil a small glass of white wine with 1 shallot and 1 garlic clove, both finely chopped, and a drop of olive oil. Add the *tellines* and cover the pan. Cook them over a high heat for about 5 minutes, shaking the pan from time to time, until they open. Alternatively simply place the washed *tellines* in a pan and cook until they open, which is better. Discard any

WINE:
Vin de Pays
rosé or
Faugères blanc

shells that remain closed. Let the *tellines* cool slightly, then mix them with the *aïoli* and serve warm.

A Picturesque Salad

~

There is another potato salad which could be the long-lost twin sister of fisherman's *rouille*. It is a similar recipe, with the same intense and luxurious flavor, but its origins are far from the Camargue—this recipe comes from Luxembourg. It may seem out of place, but never mind!

IN THE KITCHEN : Boil 2 pounds of potatoes in their skins. Brown some large cubes of bacon in a skillet over a low heat. When they are golden, but not dry, lower the heat and add 2 cups of light cream, a little wine vinegar, and a teaspoon of Dijon mustard. The sauce should have a sweet and sour taste. Season generously with freshly ground pepper. Poach a few garlic sausages (but do not forget to prick them with a fork, to prevent them from bursting) and a few frankfurters in simmering water. Then cut the sausages into thick slices. Peel the potatoes and cut them up. Mix the potatoes and the sausages with the cream and bacon sauce and serve immediately. Like the fisherman's *rouille*, this salad should be served hot.

Jérôme's Eggplant Stew

~

My good friend Jérôme is an inspired cook. He explores, experiments, researches, and rejuvenates with passion the simplest country recipes, like this one: eggplants cooked like little legs of lamb. It is one of the easiest and the prettiest of all eggplant stews.

IN THE KITCHEN : Prepare the eggplants: wash and dry them, trim off the stem end, but do not peel them. Peel about 20 garlic cloves and split them in half lengthwise. At regular intervals—about every ½ inch—insert a piece of garlic into the eggplants—as you would for a leg of lamb. Pour a little olive oil into a heavy-bottomed pan and add the eggplants. Season with sea salt or Kosher salt and freshly ground pepper. Cover and cook over a low heat for a good hour.

Broiled Peppers
and Eggplant

~

Prepare a dressing with a little olive oil, sea salt or Kosher salt, freshly ground pepper, and parsley and garlic, both finely chopped.

Light a fire of vine shoots and put a griddle over it, positioned high enough so that the flames barely touch it.

Wash and dry a few eggplants and sweet red peppers without peeling them or trimming their stems. Prick the eggplants to prevent them from bursting and broil the vegetables over the flames. They will turn completely black, but do not worry about this. Turn them over frequently so they will cook evenly on all sides.

When they are ready, peel the eggplants but do not take off the stems. Peel and seed the peppers and cut them into strips. Arrange the vegetables on a serving dish and pour the dressing over them.

You can also bake the vegetables in the oven and serve them in the same way, but you will miss out on the delicious smoky flavor—which makes all the difference— that broiling over a wood fire imparts to the vegetables.

"Lou Cachat"

~

Lou cachat is a deliciously strong, slightly pungent cheese mixture which is an ideal way of using up all the leftover bits of cheese that have dried out. To make a good cachat, just like a good vinegar, you need a "mother," which you can get from a generous friend who has a pot of cachat in their cellar and will be ready to give you some. So, once you have been given a bowlful of cachat, take a large stoneware pot with a lid. Put your "seed" cachat in it with all your leftover bits of cheese, mashed by hand or in a food processor. Pour a little white alcohol (vodka) over the top. Mix well, cover the pot, and let it stand for at least a month before tasting it. Whenever you have some leftover cheese, add it to the cheese and alcohol mixture.

WINE:
Châteauneuf
du Pape
blanc

*Broiled
Peppers and
Eggplant*

Annie Laurent's
Rice Pudding

~

First, you need to make a dark golden caramel in a flameproof mold or dish, using 20 sugar cubes and just enough water to moisten the sugar (follow the recipe on page 41). Be careful not to burn the caramel or it will taste bitter—but if it is too pale the taste of caramel will be lost. When it is golden brown but still liquid, carefully move the dish around to spread the caramel all over the sides, then let it cool.

Cook 1 cup of Camargue round rice (short-grain rice), washed and drained, in a pan of boiling water for 5 minutes. In another pan, bring 1 quart of milk to the boil with a split vanilla bean, and 3 or 4 pieces of dried orange rind. When the milk starts boiling, lower the heat and add the drained rice. Cook for 1 hour over a low heat until the milk is almost completely absorbed. The rice must still be creamy. Take the pan off the heat. Beat 4 eggs with a little sugar, but not too much because the caramel will also sweeten the pudding. Stir the rice into the eggs, remove the vanilla bean but leave the orange rind. At this point, you can

add candied fruit and golden raisins, but they are not essential. Pour the rice mixture into the caramelized dish and cook in a bain-marie in a preheated oven at 350° for 30-40 minutes. Let the pudding cool completely before inverting it on a serving dish. This pudding tastes even better when it is one day old.

Watermelon Jam

~

In Provence, we use a special watermelon for jam: it is oblong, with pale-green skin and even paler flesh. We call it *la meraviho*, the marvel. Do not use the round watermelon with the dark rind and red flesh with black seeds. That type of melon is only good eaten raw, when it is ripe and sweet.

IN THE KITCHEN : The day before, cut the watermelon into slices, remove the rind and seeds, and dice the flesh, then weigh it. For each 2 pounds of fruit, add 1 unwaxed lemon (sliced finely), a split vanilla bean, and 3 cups of sugar. Let all this macerate overnight.

The following day, put the fruit mixture in a preserving pan and cook for 30 minutes. Repeat this for 3 consecutive days until the fruit is translucent and the syrup thick. Let the jam cool before pouring into sterilized jars. Keep an eye on the jam when cooking it, because it has a tendency to foam and could easily boil over. Like fig jam (see page 165) and green tomato jam (see page 33), this is a perfect dessert jam, served with cookies or fresh cheese.

"Carthagène"

~

In Provençal, we say *Cartagèno*. This drink is a deep amber color and is served as an aperitif or as a dessert wine. Historically *Carthagène* is a royal drink, and in Arles it traditionally accompanies the 13 "desserts" served on Christmas Eve (see page 70).

If you are offered some *Carthagène* in Camargue, consider it an honor.

IN THE KITCHEN : At grape-picking time, mix 3 quarts of fresh white grape juice with 1 quart of new grape alcohol (about 60° proof). Let the mixture ferment at least until All Saints' Day (1 November), then store it in a cold cellar for a year. At the end of a year, filter it and bottle it, sealing each bottle carefully. *Carthagène* wine improves with age.

Bouillabaisse in an Artist's Studio

There is THE *bouillabaisse*, which is made with fish, and then there are all the other varieties, which use eggs, spinach, sardines, green peas, salt cod, and goodness knows what else. They are not as famous, but they are always delicious, served with toasted bread and shredded cheese, which melts in the hot soup. The variations are more common inland, where people could not get fish or were too poor to buy it. They smell beautifully of fennel and saffron, but they do not have much in common with the true *bouillabaisse*.

The name comes from the Provençal words *boui-abaisso*, meaning, in the words of the Provençal poet, Frédéric Mistral: "*boui*, the pot is boiling, *abaisso*, turn the heat down because you only need a little simmering to cook this dish." There is another explanation for the name, which describes the squatting (*abaissée*) position of the fishermen around the wood fire on which the pot is boiling, because in the olden days, this peasant soup was prepared on the beach.

But today, thanks to the marvels of refrigeration, you can find fresh fish everywhere in Provence, so you can make *bouillabaisse* anywhere. And so, I invite you to a painter's lunch to taste his special recipe.

The table is set by a window overlooking the garden. All around us large canvasses are stacked up or set up on easels. A large trolley covered with pots and brushes will serve as a side-table for piles of plates and napkins. Everything, the cooking and the eating, will take place in the studio. For the occasion we will give up working with paints to concentrate on the *bouillabaisse*; we will exchange the brush for the wooden spoon, and the fish will marinate alongside tubes and pots of paint. Meanwhile, we will have a drink of *pastis* or chilled white wine from Cassis, and we will nibble on *poutargue* (salted fish eggs) or anchovy toast, or on little fried ravioli, the way Françoise makes them. The subtle aroma of saffron mingles with the fennel, garlic, and fresh fish. The *bouillabaisse* is almost ready and the rockfish soup is already steaming in the strange soup bowl from Vallauris, a glazed bowl in the shape of a *rascasse* (scorpion fish) with elegantly made-up doe eyes. Next to a plaster Hercules, a magnificent bowl of snow cream (floating islands) is waiting near a plate of homemade biscuits which we will eat later on . . .

But we are still having our aperitifs and we have had to toast a basketful of thin slices of bread. The toast will be spread with solidified olive oil and grated *poutargue,* or tapenade (olive paste), or with the poor man's sauce (anchovy and almond sauce).

Solidified Olive Oil
and Grated "Poutargue"

~

Poutargue is the caviar of Provence. It is the eggs of the gray mullet, a fish which used to come and breed in Lake Berre. Unfortunately, there are no gray mullet left in Lake Berre, so no more real *poutargue* in Martigues. But you can get *poutargue* from north Africa—not as good, old people will tell you, but still delicious. The fish eggs, still in their original pouch, are salted, then pressed and dried. These days, they are covered with a thin film of wax or paraffin.

IN THE KITCHEN : Remove the layer of wax and the thin skin which protects the eggs, then grate them, using a Parmesan grater.

The day before, or at least a few hours before, you will have filled a bowl with very fruity extra-virgin olive oil, and will have put this bowl in the freezer so that the oil will solidify. When ready, spread it on thin slices of toast, as you would butter, and sprinkle generously with the grated *poutargue*. Eat it quickly before the oil melts.

Black Tapenade

~

Whether ripe (black) or green, tapenade does not take its name from the olive, which is nevertheless the main ingredient, but from the caper, which is called *tapeno* in Provençal. So strictly speaking, it is a caper spread.

The best olives for making black tapenade are those from Nyons.

IN THE KITCHEN : Pit 10 ounces of ripe olives and chop them finely. Put them in a mortar with 12 anchovy fillets, which have been rinsed in fresh water, and a large tablespoon of capers. Mash all the ingredients together thoroughly, using a wooden pestle. Add a dash of olive oil and a few drops of lemon juice. You will need 1 anchovy fillet and 3 capers for every 10 olives. Serve with small pieces of toasted bread.

Some people grind a little pepper into their tapenade, and that is not a bad idea.

Other people replace the lemon juice in the basic tapenade recipe with 1 tablespoon of rum. I personally prefer the lemon juice. Others also add half a mashed garlic clove. It is simply a question of how you like your tapenade to taste.

Green Tapenade
~

Take 8 ounces of pitted green olives, finely chopped, and 1 cup of blanched almonds. Using a pestle and mortar, mash the nuts and the olives together with 1 large tablespoon of capers, 6 anchovy fillets, a dash of olive oil, and, why not, if you like, add a dash of old marc brandy.

Anchovy Quichets (Toast)
~

Wash 6 large anchovies under running water and then fillet them. Using a pestle and mortar, mash them with 1 garlic clove and a little olive oil. Spread this paste on small thin slices of bread and lightly toast these *quichets* in a hot oven for 5 minutes. Serve warm.

Almond and Garlic Sauce
~

Using a pestle and mortar, crush about 30 blanched almonds with 5 garlic cloves. Add a few drops of water, then little by little add some olive oil until the paste has thickened and is smooth. Serve on toasted bread.

Almond and Anchovy Sauce

~

Frédéric Mistral used to call this the poor man's sauce, because a small piece of bread spread with this paste would make a complete meal.

Using a pestle and mortar, mash about 30 almonds or walnut halves with a few anchovy fillets and some sprigs of fennel. Add a few drops of water, then some olive oil, until the paste is thick and smooth. Serve spread on toast, or as a dip for batons of raw vegetables, such as carrots, celery, fennel bulb, or cauliflower, as for the *anchoïade* sauce (see recipe on page 141).

Fried Ravioli

~

Buy some little ravioli like those from the market at Romans—the tiny ones filled with *brousse* cheese. They are generally poached for a few seconds in chicken broth, but my friend, Françoise, when she invites us to her beautiful château in the Alpille Hills, likes to serve them fried, as a snack with drinks.

IN THE KITCHEN : Separate the ravioli carefully and fry them in a skillet in ½ inch of hot, but not smoking, olive oil, just long enough to give them a nice golden color. Remove the ravioli with a slotted spoon and drain on paper towels. Then salt them generously and serve them right away, piping hot.

Bouillabaisse from the Villepontoux Restaurant

~

There is not one, but a thousand ways of making *bouillabaisse*. Some people add leeks. Others add potatoes. Each area, each family even, has its own secret recipe. In Marseilles, on the old coast road—old *Marseillais* will remember it—there was a restaurant right in the middle of Prophet's Bay—*Le Villepontoux*. It was the restaurant owned by Elie and Jeanne Drouillet, my friend Gérard Drouillet's parents. They used to serve a *bouillabaisse* famous throughout the district and even beyond. I have often eaten this *bouillabaisse* at the table of my friend "Queen Jeanne," and it is unbeatable. It is this *bouillabaisse* recipe that I am going to share with you now. There are 3 stages and this recipe will serve about 6 people.

IN THE KITCHEN: *La soupe de poissons de roche* (rockfish soup):
First, you make a delicious soup with *poissons de roche*. In a large saucepan, heat 1 tablespoon of olive oil and cook the flesh of 2 large tomatoes for about 5 minutes with 2 sprigs of fennel, a bay leaf, 2 peeled and lightly crushed garlic cloves, a piece of dried orange rind, some saffron, salt, and freshly ground pepper. Add 3 pounds of *poissons de roche*. These are small Mediterranean fish of various species that live among the rocks along the coast. (There is no precise equivalent outside France, but you could use trimmings from fish, including pompano, halibut, red snapper, bay scallops, clams, mussels, and shrimp.) *Poissons de roche* are used whole and do not need cleaning. Cover with 2 quarts of cold water, bring to a boil, then lower the heat and simmer for 45 minutes. Pour the soup through a fine strainer, pressing well on the fish to extract all the juices.

If you are serving this soup on its own, pour it into warmed soup bowls and serve with garlic croûtons, some shredded cheese, and some *rouille* sauce or sea urchin *rouille* (see page 130).

The *bouillabaisse*:
To continue with the *bouillabaisse*, you will need really fresh fish:
— 6 monkfish steaks
— 6 conger eel steaks
— 3 weevers
— 1 John Dory
— 4 medium scorpion fish, the famous *rascasse*
You can substitute pompano, halibut and red snapper for fish that are unobtainable.

WINE: Cassis blanc

Marinating the bouillabaisse

Clean and scale all the fish, reserving their livers. Now we are going to make a marinade, and this is undoubtedly the secret of this particular recipe. Place all the fish in a large dish with some sprigs of fennel, some tomatoes and potatoes, both peeled and sliced, some salt, freshly ground pepper, and saffron. Pour over a little olive oil, mix well and let the fish marinate for a few hours in a cool place. Bring the rockfish soup to a boil. As soon as it starts boiling, add the potatoes with all the marinade, but not the fish. Return to a boil, lower the heat, and simmer for 10 minutes. Then add the firm-fleshed fish—the monkfish, the scorpion fish, and the conger eel. After 10 more minutes, lower the heat, and add the soft-fleshed fish—the John Dory and the weever. Cook for a further 5 minutes. Taste and adjust the seasoning as required. As a first course, serve the broth with garlic croûtons, shredded cheese, and sea urchin *rouille*. As a second course, serve the fish with the potatoes, a spoonful of sea urchin *rouille*, and some more broth to moisten the fish.

The *rouille*:

This owes its name to the color given to it by the sweet red peppers from Spain. Using a pestle and mortar, mash 3 garlic cloves and 3 chopped Spanish sweet red peppers. Add a walnut-size piece of bread, which you have moistened with fish soup, then squeezed dry. When the bread is blended into the garlic and pepper paste, slowly beat in some olive oil, a drop at a time, until the sauce thickens. When the *rouille* is thick and firm (like a mayonnaise), you can serve it as it is, or add a small ladle of broth from the *bouillabaisse* and present it in a gravyboat.

Sea Urchin *rouille*:

Sea urchin *rouille* is not as strong in flavor as traditional *rouille*, and I think it is delicious. You will need 5 tablespoons of sea urchin coral. First, plunge the reserved fish livers into the hot soup for 2 minutes, and then drain them well. Now, using a pestle and mortar, mash 3 garlic cloves with the fish livers. Add 1 egg yolk (which has been kept at room temperature), a pinch of sea salt or Kosher salt, some freshly ground pepper, a few strands of saffron, and the sea urchin coral. Slowly beat in the olive oil, a little at a time, to thicken the sauce as for mayonnaise.

Fishermen's Bouillabaisse

~

This is a much simpler *bouillabaisse*, but just as authentic, and perfect to eat at the beach house. The flavorings are the same, except for saffron which is not used in this recipe (too expensive). The fish will be chosen, depending on the catch of the day, from the following: red and white scorpion fish, gurnards, John Dory, weevers, monkfish, sea bass, small rock lobster, conger eel, and even crabs. Clean and scale the fish. Cut the fish into large pieces, and marinate them for 30 minutes in a large pot with some fennel, a bay leaf, a piece of dried orange rind, 1 garlic clove (crushed), the flesh of a tomato, a leek and an onion (both roughly chopped), some salt, freshly ground pepper, and a little olive oil. Meanwhile, heat 3 quarts of water and simmer the fish that are too

small to use with the heads from the larger fish. Place the pot containing the marinade and fish pieces over a medium heat, and pour over the drained fish broth. Bring to a boil, lower the heat and simmer for about 10 minutes. It is now ready to eat.

Salt Cod Bouillabaisse

~

Soak the salt cod for 24 hours, changing the water frequently to get rid of as much salt as possible. Then poach the cod by placing it in a pan of cold water and as soon as the water starts to boil, remove the pan from the heat. Leave it to poach for about 10 minutes, then drain it, reserving the cooking water.

Skin and bone the fish. In a pot, brown 2 finely chopped onions in a little olive oil. Then add the flesh of 2 or 3 tomatoes (which has been pressed through a sieve), 6 chopped garlic cloves, a few sprigs of fennel, 2 bay leaves, a piece of dried orange rind, a little thyme, a little parsley, and some freshly ground pepper. Mix all these ingredients together with a wooden spoon and add 5 or 6 thickly sliced potatoes. Cover with the reserved poaching water from the fish, and cook over a high heat for about 30 minutes. When the potatoes are tender, lower the heat and add the pieces of cod, just long enough to heat them through. Then add a few strands of saffron. Saffron preserves its flavor and fragrance better if it is not cooked.

Place warmed plates on the table, serve the fish and potatoes in a dish and the broth in warmed soup bowls, accompanied by a bowl of *aïoli* (see recipe on page 184), a bowl of shredded cheese, and some garlic toast.

WINE: Bandol rosé

One-eyed Bouillabaisse
~

Finely slice 2 leeks and 1 onion. In a heavy-bottomed pan heat 1 tablespoon of olive oil and brown the leeks and onion. Add the finely chopped flesh of 3 tomatoes, 4 chopped garlic cloves, a few sprigs of fennel, 2 bay leaves, a piece of dried orange rind, some sea salt or Kosher salt, and some freshly ground pepper. Add 6 or 7 thickly sliced potatoes and just enough water to cover the potatoes, and cover the pan. Cook over a fairly high heat until the potatoes are tender, then lower the heat so the broth barely simmers. Add a few strands of saffron. Then, allowing 1 egg per person, break each egg into a cup and gently drop them into the broth one by one, and poach them for a few minutes. Serve in warmed soup bowls, poured over large slices of toasted bread sprinkled with shredded cheese.

Stuffed "Capon"

~

I got this recipe from a fisherman in Sainte-Maxime. In this part of the world, a *chapon* (capon) is not the large fowl that we roast for Christmas, it is a beautiful red fish, a type of large *rascasse*. You will need to ask your fishmonger to fillet the fish through its back. He will have to open up the fish along the dorsal fin, sliding his knife along both sides of the backbone, snapping it at the base of the head to allow it to be removed, along with the entrails. Then prepare the stuffing: finely chop ¾ pound of white fish, ¾ pound of cooked ham, ¾ cup of pitted ripe olives, and 1 garlic clove. Add a little olive oil, a pinch of salt—but sparingly because the ham and the olives are already salted—and some freshly ground pepper. Bind with 1 egg yolk and mix well.

Stuff the fish with this mixture and tie it up with kitchen twine so that it will keep its round shape. Insert bay leaves between the twine and the fish, place it in a baking dish and drizzle a couple of tablespoons of olive oil over it. Bake it in a preheated oven at 350° for about 1¼ hours, maybe longer, depending on the size of the fish. The stuffing must be cooked through. Baste from time to time during cooking, and serve hot.

WINE:
Cassis
blanc

Snow Cream
(Floating Islands)

~

We are going to make this custard with 8 eggs and 1 quart of milk. Separate the whites from the yolks, keeping only 5 egg whites.

In a bowl, beat the yolks with 7 tablespoons of sugar until the mixture is smooth and pale.

In a pan, heat the milk. Beat the egg whites with a pinch of salt until very stiff, and then poach tablespoons of egg white, a few at a time, in the simmering milk, until they are set, about 2 minutes on each side. Remove with a slotted spoon and drain well. Place them in a pretty serving dish.

Make a caramel with 20 sugar cubes and a little water (see recipe on page 41). Lightly pour one-third of the caramel onto the poached egg whites in the dish, taking care not to damage them. Strain

Pages 134-135:
Crunchy Almond Cookies,
Shortbread, Rock Cookies
and Snow Cream

the milk and mix with the remaining caramel. Then, stirring constantly, gradually pour the hot milk onto the yolk and sugar mixture.

Return the mixture to the cleaned pan and place the pan over a very low heat; cook the custard, stirring constantly, until it thickens slightly. Do not let it boil or the custard will curdle. Pour the custard into the dish around the floating islands, and let it cool. Chill in the refrigerator for an hour before serving.

Rock Cookies
~

In a bowl, mix 2 cups of sugar and 1 stick (4 ounces) of softened butter. Add 4 cups of all-purpose flour all at once and mix well. In another bowl, whisk 1 cup of milk with 1 egg, 1 teaspoon of baking soda, and a little vanilla extract to taste. Slowly add the milk to the flour and sugar mixture and blend without working the dough too much—it should stay lumpy. Drop tablespoons of dough onto buttered baking sheets, and cook these little rocks for 15-20 minutes in a preheated oven at 350°F until firm and golden brown.

Shortbread
~

In a bowl, mix 1¾ cups of all-purpose flour, ½ cup of sugar, 1 egg, 1 teaspoon of baking powder, 3 tablespoons of milk, 7 tablespoons of melted butter, and the grated rind of 1 orange. Mix quickly, and roll the dough out until it is ¼ inch thick. With a glass, cut out rounds of dough. Place these on buttered baking sheets, brush with milk and cook for 15 minutes in a preheated oven at 350°F.

Crunchy
Almond Cookies

~

Provençal grandmothers know how to make two kinds of pale golden cookies. There are those you serve in the drawing room with a glass of muscat wine, cookies for "when we have guests," like the *navettes* (see page 162) or shortbread cookies, and those for the children for afternoon tea or dessert, like crunchy almond cookies or rock cookies. We used to call these crunchy almond cookies tooth-breakers, and as a matter of fact, they are extremely hard, but try dipping them in a glass of wine. . .

IN THE KITCHEN : First, make a syrup with 1¼ cups of sugar and 7 tablespoons of water. Let it cook slowly, stirring constantly until it reaches the thread stage (see page 31). Take the pan off the heat, pour the syrup into a large bowl, and stir in 2½ cups of blanched almonds. Let them soak in the syrup for 4 hours. At the end of that time, carefully place 4 cups of all-purpose flour on a smooth surface—a marble slab would be ideal. Make a well in the center of the flour and pour in the syrup with the almonds. Add 4 eggs and a pinch of salt. Work the dough first with your fingertips, then knead it lightly until it is smooth. Roll it until it is ½ inch thick, then cut it into strips 8 inches long by 1¼ inches wide. Place the strips on a buttered baking sheet and bake them for 20 minutes in a preheated oven at 350°F. Remove from the oven, and a few minutes later, when they have cooled slightly, cut them up into smaller strips measuring ½ by 1¼ inches. Leave them to cool completely, and store in an airtight tin.

A PICNIC ON THE BANKS
OF THE RIVER SORGUE

Springing from the rocks at Fontaine-de-Vaucluse, the River Sorgue flows, fresh and clear, through the Comtat plain then divides into several streams around l'Isle-sur-la-Sorgue. The magic starts where the streams appear. The sun shines brightly and its rays penetrate the deep shade of the large plane trees to speckle the waters of the Sorgue streams. There, beside the clear water, in the soft magic of the trees, we often go and have lunch on the grass. Every picnic starts with a large basket. We have never had one of those splendid wicker picnic hampers that one can admire in the Manufrance catalogue: large compartments stacked with china secured with leather straps, with forks on one side and knives on the other, bottles encased in wicker holders and even a small portable stove in an enamel case. We have never owned such a treasure. We use a large basket with one handle, so heavy when laden that we need two people to carry it. In it, we pack up the tablecloth and the napkins, the china and the cutlery, the bottles of wine and water and the food.

A picnic is a time to escape totally from the normal family routine: no dining room, no set places at the table, and hands, rather than forks, are used to pick up the food. Even when a column of ants marches across the tablecloth, we sit back and, slightly bemused, we watch them walk on by. Nevertheless, a picnic has its own rituals. For example, the menu is always the same: a cold tomato omelet or an *anchoïade* dip to start with, then a terrine of rabbit or beef in jelly, a noodle salad, a few goats' cheeses for the grown-ups, and a box of *Vache-Qui-Rit* (Laughing Cow) cheese spread for the children, then for dessert a pie and some fruit, or a cherry *clafoutis* in the spring.

L'anchoïade

139

The Irreplaceable Tomato Omelet

~

To make a tomato omelet, you need a concentrated *coulis*. The tomato *coulis* is one of the key sauces in Provençal cooking. This Provençal word, which has been integrated into the French cooking vocabulary, means "liquid purée." It is used to refer to either a plain tomato preserve, without any seasoning, which replaces fresh tomatoes when they are out of season (see recipe on page 159) or a tomato sauce cooked in olive oil and flavored with onions or garlic, thyme or basil, black pepper or chiles. There is not one but thousands of recipes, each one for a different use.

In the kitchen : In 1 tablespoon of olive oil, soften 2 or 3 finely chopped onions without browning them. Add a few very ripe, well-flavored tomatoes, washed, dried, and seeded, then cut into large pieces. Add 2 finely chopped garlic cloves, a little parsley, a little basil, a little thyme, a pinch of sea salt or Kosher salt, some freshly ground pepper, and 1 sugar cube. Cover and cook over a very low heat for at least 2 hours. You need to stir the *coulis* from time to time so it will not stick to the base of the

Omelet flippers

saucepan. When it has reduced and is a nice, deep, red color, you can make the omelet.

Beat 8 eggs lightly—without making them froth—and then stir in a pinch of sea salt or Kosher salt, some freshly ground pepper, and 5 to 6 tablespoons of the *coulis*. If you are cooking for a lot of people you will need to make 2 omelets. Cook the omelet in a skillet with a little olive oil over a medium heat. When it is cooked on one side, flip it over—either by sliding it onto a large saucepan lid or, if you have one, onto an omelet flipper (see illustration, above)—and cook the other side. Leave the omelet to cool.

L'anchoïade

~

L'anchoïade is an anchovy sauce. Use anchovies that have been preserved in salt, wash them under cold running water, and fillet them; about 10 anchovies will be enough for this sauce. Mash the anchovy fillets with a fork and place them in a skillet with ½ cup of olive oil, 1 tablespoon of vinegar, and some freshly ground pepper. Some people add garlic to this sauce but I find it alters the taste of the anchovies. Cook the sauce over a very low heat so the anchovies slowly dissolve in the oil without ever boiling. This will take about 15 minutes—do remember to stir constantly.

At home, this sauce is served hot with batons of raw vegetables. For the picnic, it will be transported cold in a screw-top jar. It is delicious with carrots, scallions, celery, fennel (choose the rounder female bulbs, which are more tender than the male ones), or cauliflower.

Rabbit Terrine

~

First, you will have to bone a large rabbit, leaving the pieces of meat as large as possible. Marinate the meat for at least 3 hours with a small glass of cognac, some fresh tarragon, some sea salt or Kosher salt, and freshly ground pepper. Then drain the meat carefully, reserving the marinade.

Meanwhile, grind together 1¼ pounds of boneless pork, 1¼ pounds of veal and ½ pound of bacon. Season with a little fresh tarragon, some sea salt or Kosher salt, and freshly ground pepper. Add the juice from the marinade. Bind the meats with 1 egg yolk.

Line the base and sides of a deep terrine dish—preferably one with a lid—with thin, wide slices of pork fat or bacon. Cover with a layer of ground meats, then a layer of rabbit meat, alternating the layers until the terrine is full. End with a layer of the ground meats.

Cover the top with some more pork fat or bacon and make a hole in the center.

Pages 142-143:
An island in the
River Sorgue

Cover with the lid—or with a double thickness of aluminum foil—and bake in a bain-marie in a preheated oven at 350° for about 1½ hours. When the terrine is cooked, take it out of the oven, remove the lid and weigh the meat down with a little wooden board and a weight of about 8 ounces—or a can. This will make the pâté set with a good, firm texture.

This terrine will keep in the refrigerator for 2 or 3 months, but you will have to cover it with a ½ inch layer of lard. Anyway, it is better after a few days.

Rabbit Sausage with Olives

~

WINE:
Côtes
du Ventoux
rosé

To make this delicious sausage, finely grind together ¾ pound of veal, ¾ pound of boneless pork, 15 bacon slices, 2 cups of pitted ripe olives, and 3 garlic cloves. Bone a 3 pound rabbit and dice the meat. Combine the rabbit meat with the olive mixture and add 1 small glass of cognac, 2 tablespoons of olive oil, some sea salt or Kosher salt, and freshly ground pepper (do not be stingy with the salt and freshly ground pepper—this sausage needs to be well seasoned). Let the mixture stand for 2 hours. Then bind with 2 whole beaten eggs.

Sew a piece of cloth into a 6 x 20 inch bag and fill it with the meat mixture. Make sure the meat is firmly packed and sew up the opening. In a fish pan or a large cooking pot, make a broth with just enough water to cover the rabbit sausage, some coarse salt or Kosher salt, a few peppercorns, a bouquet garni (made with the green part of a leek, some bay leaves, a sprig of thyme, a stick of celery, a sprig of parsley, and a little sage), 2 carrots, 1 onion, studded with 3 cloves, and a split calf's foot for the jelly. Put the rabbit sausage in when the broth starts boiling, then lower the heat and simmer gently for 3 hours. Remove the sausage from the broth and let it cool completely before taking it out of the cloth bag. Scoop out the vegetables and herbs and let the broth reduce for a little longer, leaving in the calf's foot. Strain the broth and put it in a cool place to let it set.

Serve the rabbit sausage sliced and garnished with cubes of jelly and ripe olives.

Olive Bread

~

This olive bread, perfect for a picnic, is also delicious served as an *hors d'oeuvre* with an aperitif.

In a bowl, mix together, in the following order, 2½ cups of all-purpose flour, 2 teaspoons of baking powder, ½ teaspoon of fine salt, 1 cup of pitted green olives, ¼ pound of diced ham, 1¼ cups of shredded Gruyère cheese, 3 eggs, a scant cup of Muscat de Beaumes-de-Venise (fragrant sweet white wine), and ⅔ cup of olive oil. Line a rectangular cake pan with buttered nonstick baking parchment. Pour the batter into the pan and bake it in a preheated oven at 325° for 45 minutes. The bread is cooked when a knife blade inserted in the center comes out clean.

Unlike the fruit cake on page 50, this olive bread is best eaten fresh on the day it is made. But let it cool before you serve it! You should get about 10 slices of olive bread from this recipe.

Chilling the wine in the river

Beef Daube
in Jelly

~

Cut 4 pounds of *galinette* into large cubes, the size of an egg (this charming and efficient geometry comes straight from my grandmother Athalie's cooking notebook). *Galinette* is the regional name for beef shank.

In the bottom of the *daubière*, or cooking pot, place a few pieces of pork rind, a few cubes of bacon, a small pat of butter, and 1 tablespoon of olive oil, then the pieces of beef shank, and a calf's foot, split in half, a sliced carrot, a few pieces of dried orange rind, and a bay leaf, and 3 or 4 garlic cloves, peeled and quartered. Season with sea salt or Kosher salt—but not too much, because of the bacon—and freshly ground pepper. Pour over a good, dry white wine until the meat is completely covered. Put the lid on the pot and simmer over a very low heat for 5 hours. When the *daube* is cooked, carefully remove the pieces of meat and set on one side. Strain the juices and skim all the fat carefully.

Pour 2 ladles of the cooking juices into a deep terrine dish. Place the terrine in the freezer for a few minutes to allow the jelly to set. Arrange the meat on top of the layer of jelly, then pour in the rest of the juices. Cover with a piece of aluminum foil and put the terrine in the refrigerator for a few hours so the jelly will set.

Lumache Pasta Salad
~

One day we were going on an impromptu picnic and I did not have much time to prepare the lunch basket, so I improvized and created this delicious and rather rustic salad with the leftovers from the refrigerator and the cupboard. From the day before, I had a *tian* of chickpeas and some green beans. I added half a packet of cooked pasta shells, the ones we call "elbows" *(lumache)* in Provence, and a few tomatoes. This cold salad was such a success that it is now *de rigueur* every time we have a picnic.

IN THE KITCHEN : You will need lots of fruity extra-virgin olive oil in which you will mix 1 teaspoon of Dijon mustard and 2 tablespoons of wine vinegar. Add a few scallions, finely chopped, ½ pound of *lumache* pasta (cooked *al dente*), ½ pound of cooked green beans (they should still be crunchy), and 1 cup of cooked chick-peas. (These should have been soaked the night before and cooked for 2 hours in salted water, unless you happen to have some spinach cooking liquid, see page 74. In that case, it would not be necessary to soak them, and 1 hour of cooking time would be enough.) Add 2 firm tomatoes, washed, dried and quartered, a few capers, and, finally, a few curls of dry goats' cheese. Leave all these ingredients piled up in your salad bowl. Cover with foil for the trip. Just before serving, mix the salad.

Lumache
Pasta Salad

Beef Daube

~

If you would like a winter *daube*, nice and hot and served with fresh pasta or brown rice from Camargue, the recipe is almost the same as for the beef *daube* in jelly (see recipe on page 145). Use beef chuck instead of shank. Omit the calf's foot, which was only there for the jelly, use 6 or 7 unpeeled garlic cloves, and halve the quantity of wine. Everything else is the same!

One more delightful piece of advice from my grandmother: "If you want a more economical and more abundant dish, 45 minutes before serving time, cut some carrots into thick slices and cook them in boiling salted water with a garlic clove and an onion. "At the last minute, add the carrots (without the garlic clove and onion) to the *daube*, along with some ripe olives. Mix well."

Nanie's Cake

~

Here is a recipe I learned from my mother, a cake for when you want something quick to make for a snack or a picnic. For each large egg you need 6 tablespoons of all-purpose flour, 6 tablespoons of sugar, 3 tablespoons of milk, 4 tablespoons of melted butter, ¾ teaspoon of baking powder and the grated rind of 2 lemons for flavor. A 4-egg quantity works well.

Mix all these ingredients together in a bowl. Pour the batter into a buttered, deep cake pan, and bake for 20 minutes in a preheated oven at 350°F.

Cherry
Clafoutis

~

I love this delicious *clafoutis*, which is made with dark, ripe cherries, but you can make it with other kinds of fruit at different times of the year (peaches in summer, pears and figs in the fall, or apples in winter).

Liberally butter a porcelain or earthenware dish, then add a layer of the cherries, without stems but not pitted, up to 1¼ inches deep. In a separate bowl, mix 5 tablespoons of flour with 5 tablespoons of sugar and a pinch of salt. Add 4 tablespoons of milk, little by little, whisking well all the time to avoid lumps. Add 5 eggs, one at a time. Pour the mixture over the fruit and cook for 15 minutes in a preheated oven at 350°. Then take the dish out of the oven and sprinkle the *clafoutis* with sugar and dots of butter. Put the *clafoutis* back in the oven for a another 10 minutes. Serve warm or cold.

A Day at the "Cabanon"

Our *cabanon* (cabin) is beside a creek, very close to Marseilles. Early in the morning, before catching the boat at *le Vieux-Port*, the Old Harbor, you will need to buy some fish, unless you are absolutely sure you are going to catch your own. We climb on board the boat, loaded like donkeys with food and bottles of water and wine. After the 15-minute boat ride, we have to walk along a stony path carrying our heavily laden baskets. Finally we arrive at the *cabanon*, the rocks, the sea, the beauty, and the freedom of it all!

While some of us are fishing for sea urchins, others are getting the coals ready and Auntie Anne is making the sauce for the pasta. Auntie Anne is a genuine *Marseillaise*, a girl from the Saint-Jean neighborhood (here, we say a *San Janenque*). She is the grand-daughter of a fishwife from *le Vieux-Port* who, one day, stepped off the boat from Naples and stayed. And that is why the cooking of Marseilles sometimes has an Italian flavor, or so we say in our family. Two years ago, at the Christmas *santons* fair, at the top of the Canebière in Marseilles, a new *santon* figurine made an appearance. Alongside the ox and the donkey, Grasset and Grasseto, the blind man, and the pistachio seller, was the *pizzaiolo*, a Neapolitan immigrant who had at last become a true Provençal. This is only fair, since pizza has been a national dish of Provence for such a long time now.

But back to the *cabanon*. The coals are almost ready and the sea bream is patiently wait-ing on its griddle. Deep inside the cooking pot, *le monstre* (octopus) is cooking in the

Spaghetti "au monstre" in the shade of the "cabanon"

steam from the garlic and tomato. On the terrace, the children are setting the table. Talking about the table, this one is a very peculiar construction of boards and marbled vinyl tiles with two rather strange unmatched chairs. There is an actual style of *cabanon* furniture, one could almost call it *cabanon* art, made up of oil cans and broken plates, masses of ingenuity, and incredible audacity when it comes to taste! In the *calanques* (creeks) of Cassis, from the Goudes to *la pointe Rouge*, around Malmousque, in the *vallon des Auffes*, from the Estaque to Martigues, and all around Lake Berre, hundreds of *cabanons* bear witness to the fabulous creativity of their builders. There, in a stony environment, with sparse vegetation due to lack of fresh water and the salty vapors of the sea, they have erected these amazing shacks, often made from the garbage collected from the nearby city. But whether they have been prettily arranged or stand proud in their plainness, all of them, in their simplicity or their folly, are dedicated to pleasure and laziness.

Sea Urchins

~

This time we are going to start our meal with a platter of sea urchins, and I have some advice on how to fish for them. Even if you can find beautiful sea urchins at a good fishmonger, the pleasure of eating them is far greater when you have caught them yourself and can savor them on the spot.

Like oysters and mussels, you do not fish for sea urchins from May to September, the period of reproduction. But we are in April, the weather is glorious, and the sea is calm; never mind if the urchins are not quite as perfect as in February. Plastic sandals are necessary because sea urchin spines are very painful. Take along a canvas potato sack to store your catch and a pail with a glass bottom, which we call *une glace* (a mirror) around here, to be able to see the sea bed clearly. You can also arm yourself with an old fork, which will be helpful to scrape the urchins off the rocks if you are worried about your fingers. Personally, I prefer to use my hands, and with a little practice it is perfectly safe. On the rocks, you will see urchins of all kinds and colors. All the small ones, purple, blue, red, or green, are good, but do not take the big black ones. They will be empty and will be a waste of time and effort. When you bring them back to the *cabanon*, you leave them in the wet canvas bag until lunchtime, taking care to keep the bag moist.

Open the sea urchins at the very last minute, and to do that you will need to sacrifice a pair of old kitchen scissors which you will not be able to use for anything else afterward! Cut an opening at the base of the shell, around the mouth. Be careful not to damage the coral inside. Once you have done 2 or 3 urchins, you will have the knack. You can pour out the sea water and scrape off the brown bits to leave only the red coral, but true *aficionados* eat everything.

Eat your sea urchins as soon as they are ready, with little sticks of bread, the way you would eat a soft-boiled egg. Do not add lemon juice or vinegar: the flavor of the urchins is perfect on its own.

French Fries,
Vinsobres Style

~

WINE:
Vinsobres
rouge

People who have never tasted my friend Hélène's French fries cannot understand how on earth large potato sticks cooked in a skillet of olive oil can taste so good. The secret is simple and Hélène agreed to share it with me. Wash and peel 6 or 7 large potatoes and cut them into thick sticks. Heat ½ inch of olive oil in a large skillet over a medium heat. Dry the potato sticks thoroughly before adding them to the oil (which should be hot, but not smoking). Cooking must be slow, the oil bubbling around the potatoes, which will gradually acquire a nice golden color. If the oil is too hot, they will darken too quickly without being cooked. If the oil is not hot enough, the potato sticks will absorb too much fat and will remain pale and limp. As they change color, turn them carefully with a fork to let them brown evenly on all sides.

The real secret comes after about 10 minutes: throw into the pan at least a dozen unpeeled garlic cloves and let them cook alongside the potato sticks, constantly turning them over. This causes a strange alchemy which imparts to the potato not only flavor but also a particular texture which is like no other. When the French fries are nicely crusty and golden, transfer them to a serving dish lined with paper towels. Season generously with sea salt or Kosher salt, tossing the French fries in the dish to distribute the salt evenly. Serve immediately.

Personally, I do not know of any French fries that taste better than these. As a matter of fact, they are a dish on their own, ideal as a first course or with a green salad, even though they also make a perfect accompaniment to broiled fish or meat.

Sea urchins

The Baron's
Sea Bream

~

Our baron is from Toulon and he is a fisherman. In fact, I should call him a gardener of the sea, because he goes to sea the way you have a walk around the garden, and always brings back fish for the meal, fish so fresh that it still wriggles in his basket. The recipe is rustic and easy, so its success will rely on the freshness and quality of the fish. The royal sea bream is of course a fish fit for kings, but other members of the bream family will do just as well for this recipe.

IN THE KITCHEN : Prepare a good fire with vine stumps or cuttings.

Scale a sea bream and clean it out well, but do not wash it; wipe it carefully.

Season the inside of the fish with sea salt or Kosher salt and freshly ground pepper, and stuff with slices of fennel and a handful of sage leaves. Let it stand for a while.

In a bowl, make a vinaigrette with sea salt or Kosher salt, freshly ground pepper, olive oil, and a little vinegar.

Make a little brush by tying a bunch of fresh sage leaves to a wooden stick about 12 inches long. This brush will be used to baste the bream with the vinaigrette while it is cooking. You will have to baste it often so it does not dry out. That is the secret of this recipe.

Place the fish in a hinged broiler and let it cook over the hot coals for about 10 minutes on each side. To check if the fish is cooked, test with the tip of a knife between the gill and the backbone. The cooking time will depend, of course, on the size of the fish.

When the fish is ready, throw the sage brush into the fire, because you will not be able to use it again.

The bream can also be baked in the oven and will still be delicious.

Serve it with fennel and tomatoes (see recipe on page 158).

WINE : Coteaux d'Aix en Provence blanc

A sage brush

Fennel and Tomatoes

~

This is the perfect accompaniment for our bream. In a heavy-bottomed pan, heat a little olive oil and gently cook 2 roughly chopped onions and a handful of diced bacon until the onions are soft. Add 6 large fennel bulbs, cut in half, 5 or 6 unpeeled garlic cloves, a glass of dry white wine, and some sea salt or Kosher salt and freshly ground pepper. Simmer for 10 minutes, then add 6 ripe tomatoes, chopped, or a jar of preserved tomatoes (see recipe on page 159).

Cover and simmer for about 1 hour, until all the flavors have combined.

Salt Cod, Grandet Style

~

Here is a recipe for lazy cooks, because, at the *cabanon*, one feels more like lazing around than cooking all day. Choose some nice salted but not dried cod fillets. Rinse the fish carefully under running water and soak it for a couple of hours only. You do not need to soak it for 24 hours, because you are going to poach it in a large quantity of water and you want it to impart its flavor and saltiness to the vegetables.

To a large cooking pot full of boiling water, add some carrots, some leeks, old potatoes, turnips, pieces of pumpkin, and fennel, all of which should have been washed, peeled, and chopped into large pieces. Add a splash of olive oil, 2 bay leaves, a few peppercorns, but no salt. Cook the vegetables for 30 minutes, and when they are tender, add the drained cod. Turn off the heat and let the fish poach in the vegetable broth for about 10 minutes. Drain and serve, drizzled with a little olive oil. The cod will still be a little salty but, eaten with the vegetables, it will be delicious.

Wine:
Coteaux d'Aix
en Provence
rosé

Tomato Preserve
and Tomato Coulis

~

It is a fact that you can now buy excellent canned tomatoes in the shops. But if you happen to be on holiday in July, when tomatoes are cheap, and you feel like savoring the pleasures of a bygone era, make some tomato preserve following these recipes. Then you can store them at the *cabanon*.

First, we will make jars of whole tomatoes. You will need firm tomatoes, not too ripe. Wash and dry them. Cut them in half and take out the seeds. Then pack the tomatoes into some sterilized glass jars and top up the jars with lightly salted water. Seal the jars and then place them in a sterilizer or large washboiler with some straw or hay around them to prevent breakages. Fill up the washboiler with cold water. Place it over the heat and bring the water to a boil. Sterilize the jars for 15 minutes, at a rolling boil.

For the *coulis*, we are going to preserve a purée of tomatoes without any seasoning. Of course, this *coulis* is not meant to be used as is. Use it in winter, when fresh tomatoes are rare, expensive, and tasteless, or as a base for delicious sauces (see recipe on page 140).

You need large ripe tomatoes. Peel and seed them (to peel them more easily, plunge them into boiling water for 2 minutes). I should add that tomato skin gives sauces a delicious flavor but is totally indigestible. Chop up the tomato flesh and cook it for 15 minutes. Then press through a fine strainer and pour it straight into some sterilized jars (in the old days, they used to keep the *coulis* in champagne bottles). Seal the jars and sterilize them (see method for tomato preserve) for 1 hour. Let them cool before taking them out of the sterilizer.

Spaghetti "au Monstre"

~

First, we are going to braise *le monstre*. *Le monstre* is a 2 or 3 pound octopus. If it is any larger, the animal will be too tough. It should not be too fresh either, because then the skin would be too tough. Ideally the octopus should be caught at least the day before and kept for up to 36 hours in the refrigerator.

First, it has to be beaten against a rock, rather hard and for quite a while (do not worry, it is dead by now) to soften the flesh. Then remove the hard beak and the innards, but not the skin.

In a large flameproof pot, lightly brown 4 peeled garlic cloves in some olive oil. Discard this garlic and add 3 pounds of ripe tomatoes, peeled and chopped (or use a jar of preserved tomatoes). Add a small hot chile and some freshly ground pepper.

Salt will be added at the end because the octopus might release some sea water while it is cooking. Cook the sauce for 20 minutes, then add the octopus. Simmer, covered, for 1-1½ hours, depending on the size of your octopus.

Check if the octopus is cooked by pricking it with a fork, which should penetrate easily. If the sauce is too runny, reduce it by boiling it, uncovered, for a little while, first removing the octopus and keeping it warm. Taste the sauce and add salt if necessary, as well as a large handful of chopped parsley.

Cook the spaghetti in a large pan of boiling salted water until *al dente*. Drain the pasta and, just before serving, toss everything together in a large bowl: the spaghetti, the sauce, and *le monstre*.

Wine:
Coteaux d'Aix en Provence, Les Baux rouge

Spaghetti "au Monstre"

Spaghetti
with Clams
~

WINE:
Palette
blanc

Pour a little olive oil into a deep, wide pan over a low heat, then slowly cook 2 chopped garlic cloves and 1 small chopped hot chile, until the garlic is golden brown. Add 2 pounds of washed clams, cover the pan, and cook over a low heat for a few minutes until the shells have opened. Discard any that remain closed. Toss the clams with 1 pound of spaghetti (cooked *al dente*) and a good handful of chopped parsley. Serve right away with some shredded cheese.

Auntie Anne's
Spaghetti with Sausage
~

WINE:
Palette
rosé

In a cast-iron pan, brown 3 garlic cloves in some peanut oil, then remove the garlic cloves and keep on one side. In the same oil, brown a few garlic sausages, a few pork cutlets, and some pieces of bacon. When they are nice and golden, take them out and keep warm. To the pan, add 2 pounds of ripe tomatoes, peeled and chopped, or a jar of tomato preserve. Return the garlic cloves to the pan, together with a few basil leaves, some sea salt or Kosher salt and freshly ground pepper, and 1 cube of sugar. Let the sauce simmer gently for 30 minutes, then put all the meats back in the pan and cook for another 15 minutes or so.

Serve with spaghetti (cooked *al dente*) with some shredded cheese.

Navettes
~

Navettes (shuttles) are pale blond cookies, flavored with orange-blossom water, in the shape of the little shuttles used by weavers in the old days. When I was a child in Aix, we used to buy them from the cookie factory on *rue des Tanneurs*. When the oven was hot, we could smell the cookies baking from the bottom of *rue des Cordeliers* to the top of *rue Espariat*. Of course, the cookie factory on *rue des Tanneurs* has long gone, but here is a rather good recipe for *navettes*.

IN THE KITCHEN : Make a syrup by boiling 7 tablespoons of water with ½ cup of sugar for 5 minutes. Let the syrup cool. In a bowl, sift 2½ cups of all-purpose flour with a pinch of salt, add 1¼ sticks (5 ounces) of softened butter and rub in until the mixture resembles fine breadcrumbs. Pour the syrup and 1 tablespoon of orange-blossom water over the mixture.

Mix well to produce a smooth and supple dough. Roll out the dough to a thickness of ⅓ inch and then use a knife to cut out 3 inch long lozenges. Make a deep slit along the length of each cookie, without cutting right to the ends. Butter some baking sheets and place the *navettes* on them. Bake for about 20 minutes in a preheated oven at 350°F. They should not brown. Let them cool completely on a wire rack before packing them into a tin and taking them to the *cabanon*.

Navettes

Brousse Cheese from Rove

~

Brousse cheese is a delicious fresh goats' cheese which has been made in Rove for as long as I can remember, on Rove Hill, close to Marseilles, between Estaque and Redonne. It is prepared in rather unusual, small containers, long and narrow, which are pierced at the bottom to allow the cheeses to drain. The containers used to be made of blown glass or woven straw. Today they are made of plastic, but this has not made any difference to the quality of the cheese.

Young goatherds used to come and sell their produce in the streets of Marseilles, and even as far as Aix. Carrying their produce in large wicker baskets which hung from their necks and blowing a little trumpet, they would shout "Brousse cheese from the Rove." I can still remember hearing them. Today there are no more street sellers in Aix, but thankfully there are still a few goats on the Rove and you can still find the cheese at good dairies and markets.

Brousse cheese is best eaten fresh with a dash of rum and some sugar, or with a good jam like the rose-hip jam (see recipe on page 55) or this fig jam.

Fig Jam

~

You should make this jam in September, when figs are sweet and plump. Actually we should call this preserve candied figs, because we are going to leave them whole. Choose figs that are firm and not too ripe. Prick each fig several times with a needle. Blanch the figs in boiling water, drain them well and place them in a preserving pan with 3 cups of sugar for every 2 pounds of fruit. Let them macerate until the following day.

Cook the figs until the syrup thickens enough to cover a wooden spoon without dripping. Add a good-size glass of rum, boil for another few minutes, then pour into sterilized jars.

The "cabanon"

LUNCH ON THE TERRACE

People here have never understood why, in the middle of August, most tourists insist on having lunch in the hot midday sun. It seems pure folly to see all those pale bodies determined to burn and turn lobster-red. In a country that has invented the afternoon siesta, not because of a natural inclination to laziness but because you have worked in the fields half the night, it is natural and refreshing to rest during the hottest part of the day. The people of Provence love the sun in winter and the shade in summer. That is why they grow trees like elm and mulberry in front of their houses to provide the necessary shade. But, later in the year, when the time has come, the trees will shed their leaves to let the light and the warmth through. This is also why often they grow a vine over a terrace on the side of their houses. They can then set a table under its shade during the warm season. Lunch on the vine-covered terrace starts rather early, around 11:30, with a drink. Feeling relaxed after a glass of homemade walnut or orange wine, your taste buds will have been nicely titillated by crispy golden fritters of zucchini blossoms and the marvelous aroma coming from *soupe au pistou* in the kitchen. This, according to *les provençaux*, is the best way to work up an appetite . . .

Orange wine served on a covered terrace

Red and white beans for "soupe au pistou"

Olga's Walnut Wine

~

In June, cut 25 whole green walnuts (including the husks) into quarters. Let them macerate in a covered jar in 1 quart of eau-de-vie (white fruit spirits) with a split vanilla bean. After a month, filter the alcohol and pour it into a demijohn (a large narrow-necked bottle with 5 quarts of red wine and 4 cups of sugar. Let the mixture age in a dark, cool place for at least 5 months, then bottle it. Seal the bottles well and wait another 6 months before tasting your walnut wine.

Orange Wine

~

You should make this wine in January. Take a large glass container with a lid. Fill it with 2 lemons, 5 sweet oranges, and 5 bitter oranges, all washed, dried, and quartered (choose unwaxed fruit). Add 5 quarts of good white wine and 1 quart of eau-de-vie (white fruit spirits). Mix in 4 cups of sugar and a split vanilla bean. Seal the container and store it in a dark cool place. After 2 months, you can decant the wine into bottles, which need to be sealed carefully. Like the walnut wine, you will have to wait at least 6 months before drinking it. Serve it chilled or with ice cubes.

Zucchini and Zucchini-Blossom Fritters

~

With your aperitif you can treat your guests to these delicious zucchini fritters and zucchini-blossom fritters. Choose smallish, very fresh, young zucchini with smooth, tender skins so you will not have to peel them. The blossoms must be firm and open.

First, make a spicy tomato *coulis*: heat a little olive oil and brown a crushed garlic clove and 1 or 2 small, hot chiles for a couple of seconds. Then add some chopped, very ripe tomatoes, a little salt, a sugar cube, and a few basil leaves. Cover and simmer over a low heat for 1 hour. When the *coulis* is ready, let it cool. You should serve it at room temperature.

Now make a fairly liquid batter by mixing some flour and water with a whisk. Season with sea salt or Kosher salt and freshly ground pepper.

Then prepare the vegetables. Remove the pistil and the stem from the blossoms and cut the zucchini in thin slices. You could also add 2 potatoes, peeled and finely sliced, if wished.

Make the fritters at the last moment: they must be served piping hot.

In a large skillet, heat at least 1 inch of peanut oil. With a fork, dip the zucchini and potato slices, if using, and the blossoms, into the batter, then immediately into the hot oil.

Brown the fritters on both sides and let them drain on paper towels on a warm plate. Serve them right away with the tomato *coulis*.

A Jar of Anchovies

~

Spring is the best time to prepare these. At the fishmongers or market, choose nice plump anchovies, absolutely fresh: the success of this recipe depends upon this. Do not wash them but wipe them carefully. Do not gut them either. In a large shallow dish, let the anchovies marinate for 3 hours in their own weight of table salt. They should be completely buried in the salt. Do not use coarse salt or Kosher salt because then you would have to salt them for a lot longer. After 3 hours, remove the anchovies from the salt, and soak them in white wine vinegar for another 3 hours. After that, you can fillet the anchovies and arrange them in a sterilized preserving jar with some chopped garlic and parsley, and cover them with good olive oil. Keep the jar in a cool place, and use the anchovies within 1 month. But do not forget to bring the jar to room temperature a few hours before serving. Eat these anchovies with bread and butter. They are a delicious feast!

Pages 170-171:
Bruno Carles' Mas de
Malherbes in
Camargue

Auntie Lilette's "Soupe au Pistou"

~

Place ½ pound of fresh white haricot beans, ½ pound of fresh red haricot beans, ¾ pound of large green beans, cut in half, 2 zucchini, 3 potatoes, cubed, and 2 white onions, roughly chopped, in a large pot with about 3 quarts of salted water. That is all. Do not be tempted to add a few carrots for color because their taste would alter the flavor of the basil in the *pistou*. Cook these vegetables gently for about 2 hours; after 1½ hours, remove all the pieces of potato and zucchini and mash them, before returning them to the pot.

Now, we are going to make the *pistou*. Cook 3 whole tomatoes in the soup for 30 minutes. Then, take them out, peel them, and let them cool in a colander. In a large marble mortar, using a wooden pestle, mash 1 large handful of fresh basil leaves with 7 garlic cloves. Then add the peeled tomatoes and 5 tablespoons of olive oil. Keep mashing. Finally, add 1¼ cups of shredded cheese. The best cheese for this soup is *le rouge* (Dutch Edam with annatto coloring) from Holland, but you can use Gruyère or Parmesan. Season generously with freshly ground pepper and mix well to make a smooth paste.

A few minutes before serving, add 3 handfuls of *lumache* (elbow) pasta to the soup. When the pasta is cooked, take the soup off the heat and let it cool a little before stirring in the *pistou*. Serve immediately, or serve it cold the following day. This thick soup is, of course, very nourishing, and since it is so delicious, one has a tendency to have a second helping. In which case it should be the main course of your meal with just a green salad to follow, then a tray of goats' cheese and a good dessert.

Radish Greens
or Nettle Soup

~

Here is a lighter and truly economical soup, which will make a delicious first course and amuse your friends. It is a spring soup, to be made when radishes are tender and nettle shoots bright green in the fields.

Either take the greens from a large bunch of radishes or go and pick a bunch of nettle shoots. If you do not touch the top of the leaves, you will not be stung; alternatively you can wear gloves. Wash the leaves and throw away the stems. In a large pan, melt a little butter, add the leaves, and cook until soft. Add 4 potatoes, washed, peeled, and finely sliced. Cover with water and season with sea salt or Kosher salt, freshly ground pepper, and freshly grated nutmeg. Simmer gently for 30 minutes.

Meanwhile, in a bowl, mix 3 tablespoons of heavy cream with 1 egg yolk. Take the pan off the heat and add a little soup to the cream and egg mixture. Then pour this mixture into the soup, stir thoroughly and serve right away.

My Mother's
Salt Cod Gratin

~

Soak the salt cod, changing the water frequently. Poach it for 15 minutes in simmering water, but do not let it boil. Remove the skin and the bones, and flake the fish.

In a flameproof gratin dish, over a low heat, heat a little olive oil and lightly brown 2 onions, the white part of 2 leeks, and 2 garlic cloves, all finely chopped. When they are golden, add the flaked fish, then cover the fish with a layer of sliced potatoes which have been parboiled. Finish with a layer of ripe tomatoes, sliced fairly thickly. Bake in a medium oven for 15 minutes. Then add a dash of olive oil and some shredded cheese. Return to the oven for a further 20 minutes or so until the gratin is golden. Take it out of the oven and let it set and cool for 5 to 10 minutes before serving.

WINE:
Côtes
du Rhône
rosé

Tian of
Glazed Eggplants

~

You will need 4 or 5 firm, medium-size eggplants, and the same number of both tomatoes and white onions, choosing vegetables with a similar diameter to the eggplants. Wash and dry the eggplants and the tomatoes, but do not peel them. Peel the onions, though. Cut all the vegetables into ¼ inch thick slices. Now arrange alternate slices in an ovenproof gratin dish—eggplant, onion, tomato, eggplant, onion, and so on. Do not layer them horizontally, but place them skin-side up (see the picture opposite). They must be packed tightly together, leaving no room in the dish.

Tuck 10 or 12 small garlic cloves among the vegetables. Sprinkle with sea salt or Kosher salt, freshly ground pepper, some fresh thyme and marjoram, and a generous helping of olive oil. Bake in a preheated oven at 350° for about 20 minutes. Then take the dish out of the oven and gently press on the vegetables with a slotted spoon, to let the juices mingle. Be careful not to crush the vegetables. Return to the oven for a further 40 minutes. If you wish, 15 minutes before the end of the cooking time, you can sprinkle some grated Dutch cheese over the top. This is delicious, but not essential.

Madame Cheynet's
Eggplant

~

Madame Cheynet was a friend of my mother's, who had adopted Provence as her home. She was a marvelous cook and to our great delight adapted an old recipe for potatoes with bacon (see recipe on page 26) by substituting the potatoes with eggplant. Here is her recipe.

Choose small eggplants, plump and squat. Wash and dry, but do not peel them.

Split them lengthwise on one side, but do not cut right through, so that the 2 halves will not be completely separated. Place a thin slice of bacon between the eggplant halves, and tie the eggplants up with some kitchen twine. Pour a little peanut oil into a cast-iron pot. Add the eggplants with a large onion, chopped, and 3-4 ripe tomatoes, cut into quarters. Season with sea

salt or Kosher salt and freshly ground pepper, but be careful not to add too much salt because of the bacon. Cover the pot and cook over a low heat for a good hour. To finish off the dish, remove the lid and cook a little longer to let any excess juices evaporate. They are delicious served warm, or even cold the following day. Remove the twine before serving the eggplants.

Zucchini Gratin
~

For 2 pounds of zucchini you will need ¾ pound of white onions. Clean the zucchini; do not peel them, but slice them. Peel and chop the onions. Cook the vegetables in boiling salted water for 30 minutes. Drain well, then mash the vegetables in a pan or flameproof gratin dish with a fork. Stir in a little butter, 1 or 2 tablespoons of all-purpose flour to bind the mixture, and 2 tablespoons of light cream. Cook for 2 or 3 minutes. Transfer, if necessary, to an ovenproof gratin dish. Sprinkle over some shredded cheese, lightly pressing it down with a fork, then sprinkle with breadcrumbs and bake for 15 minutes in a preheated oven at 350°. Unlike the *tian* of glazed eggplants, this gratin is not a dish in itself, but it is a perfect accompaniment for broiled meat or roast lamb.

Les Petits Farcis
(Stuffed Vegetables)
~

For each person, you will need 1 tomato, 1 baby eggplant, 1 small zucchini, or other small round squash, and 1 sweet green pepper. Choose pretty, plump, and round vegetables that are not too large. It is now possible to buy different varieties of squash and eggplants which would be perfect for this recipe.

Wash and dry the vegetables. Slice off the tops of the tomatoes, and use a teaspoon to remove any seeds and excess water. Cut off the tops of the peppers and carefully remove the seeds and membranes from the insides. Tail the eggplants with a sharp knife, then use a teaspoon to hollow out the centers. Make sure you do not damage the skin, and keep the flesh you are removing. Do the same with the little round squash.

Now we are going to prepare the stuffings, which will be different for each vegetable. The stuffing ingredients will be chopped separately, then mixed in a bowl with some shredded cheese, some uncooked rice (which will absorb any vegetable juice), and 2 eggs to bind everything together.

For the tomatoes: grind some leftover cooked beef from a *daube* or boiled beef. Then chop 2 garlic cloves, 1 onion, 1 tomato, peeled and seeded, and the flesh of the squash. In a skillet, brown the onion in a little olive oil, then add the garlic, the other remaining vegetables, and finally the meat. Take the pan off the heat, and add 1 cup of Camargue round rice (short-grain), 2 eggs, a handful of shredded cheese, a pinch of sugar, sea salt or Kosher salt, and freshly ground pepper.

For the eggplants: grind some leftover cooked lamb, from a roast for instance. Then chop 2 garlic cloves, 1 onion, the flesh of 2 tomatoes, and the flesh of the eggplants. Heat a little olive oil and brown the onion, then add the eggplant flesh, the garlic, and tomato. Add a handful of rice, a handful of shredded cheese, a handful of pignoli (pine nuts), 2 eggs, some sea salt or Kosher salt, and freshly ground pepper.

For the green peppers: grind some cooked ham and chop the flesh of 1 sweet red pepper and 1 tomato, 2 garlic cloves, and 1 onion. Brown the onion in a little olive oil, then add the pepper, the garlic, and the tomato. Add the ham with a handful of rice, a handful of shredded cheese, 2 eggs, and some sea salt or Kosher salt and freshly ground pepper.

For the squash: brown 1 chopped onion in a little olive oil, add 5 ounces of fresh goats' cheese (such as *brousse*), a handful of rice, a handful of shredded cheese, 2 eggs, and some freshly chopped parsley. Season with a little sea salt or Kosher salt and some freshly ground pepper.

Fill the vegetables with their respective stuffings. Arrange them side by side in a large gratin dish. Sprinkle with breadcrumbs and drizzle with olive oil. Bake in a warm oven for at least 2 hours. The vegetables must be glazed and golden at the end of the cooking time. Take *les petits farcis* out of the oven and let cool for at least 10 minutes before serving.

WINE: Côtes du Rhône rosé

Lambs' Trotters and
Tripe Bundles à la Marseillaise

~

At the tripe shop or the butchers, choose 2 lambs' bellies and 8 lambs' trotters, and a generous 1½ pounds of calf's caul. Wash these carefully under running water. Cut the bellies into rectangular pieces measuring 4 x 2 inches. Roll each piece around a piece of bacon, and tie these little bundles up with stretched strips of calf's caul. A lot of people chop up the bacon with garlic and parsley, but my grandmother Athalie never did. Neither do I, as I think this recipe is delicious as it is.

WINE:
Côtes
du Rhône
rosé

In a deep earthenware dish with a lid, arrange the lambs' trotters and the bundles in alternate layers with a mixture of sliced carrots, thinly sliced onions and shallots, peeled and chopped tomatoes, a few pieces of bacon, sliced celery, 1 or 2 finely chopped garlic cloves, and some parsley. Season with sea salt or Kosher salt and freshly ground pepper. You can add 2 to 3 cloves if you like their flavor. Pour in a glass of white wine. Make a ribbon of dough with flour and a little water and use it to seal the lid onto the dish (as long as the lid has a small hole to let the steam escape). Place the covered dish in a preheated oven at 325° and bake for 6 to 7 hours.

This is a summer recipe, using fresh tomatoes. The next recipe is for a winter dish of trotters and bundles.

Delicious Trotters
and Bundles

~

Prepare the tripe (bellies) as in the previous recipe. We are now simply going to stuff the bundles differently, by chopping together 10 bacon slices and 3½ ounces of fresh truffles, and adding ½ cup of chopped, lean, cured raw ham.

Pour a little olive oil into a flameproof pot and slowly brown 1 onion, 1 carrot, and 1 stalk of celery, all finely chopped. Arrange the trotters on these vegetables, then add the tripe bundles. Add 1 cup of tomato *coulis* (see recipe on page 159), 2 garlic cloves, 2 cloves, a little thyme, and 2 bay leaves. Moisten with 1 cup of white wine and 2 cups of broth. Season lightly with sea salt or Kosher salt and freshly ground pepper. Cover the pot, sealing the lid with a ribbon of dough, and bake in a preheated oven at 325° for 6 to 7 hours. Break the dough seal and serve.

WINE:
Hermitage
rouge

Tomatoes
à la Provençale

~

For this very simple and delicious dish, you must choose nice round tomatoes, bright red but still firm. Wash, dry, and cut them in half. Carefully remove the seeds. Cook the tomato halves, cut side down, in a skillet with a little olive oil, over a high heat. After a few minutes, turn them over and cook the other side. Lower the heat, and let them simmer for a good 10 minutes. Then transfer the tomato halves to an oiled baking dish. They should be packed fairly tightly together. Sprinkle with sea salt or Kosher salt, freshly ground pepper, and a pinch of sugar to counteract the acidity of the tomatoes. Sprinkle with chopped garlic and parsley, and finally a few breadcrumbs. Drizzle a little olive oil over the tomatoes, and bake them in a preheated oven at 350° until the tomatoes are almost caramelized.

Fig Gratin

~

In the province of Comtat, toward the end of the summer, we make a beautiful dessert with figs. For this recipe small Caromb figs are ideal, but any other variety of autumn fig, fully ripe and plump, will do. The people of Provence have adapted the classic recipe of baked apples by using figs, and it is perhaps even better.

IN THE KITCHEN : Wash and dry the figs, and tail but do not peel them. Cut a cross on the top of each fig and lightly squeeze to allow them to open a little. Arrange them in tightly packed rows, cut side up, in a gratin dish. Sprinkle with a good measure of fruit alcohol (such as pear or raspberry), and place a little pat of butter in each fig. Sprinkle with sugar and bake in a low preheated oven at 325° for at least 1½ hours.

Serve warm, but not hot, with thick fresh cream or chantilly cream (see recipe on page 196).

Apricot Gratin

~

In a large bowl, mix by hand 1 cup of all-purpose flour, 1 cup of finely ground almonds, ½ cup of sugar, and a pinch of salt. Rub in 1½ sticks (6 ounces) of butter until the mixture resembles fine breadcrumbs. Stir in ¾ cup of pignoli (pine nuts) and ¾ cup of blanched almonds. Arrange large ripe apricots, halved and stoned, cut side up, in an ovenproof gratin dish. Then simply cover the apricots with the crumble mixture and bake for 1 hour in a preheated oven at 325°. Serve warm.

Fig Gratin and
Apricot Gratin

A Garden Feast

Today is a day of celebration in the big pink house. Yesterday, the aunties and children went to the woods to gather branches of box (an evergreen shrub) for their dark-green table garlands. And this morning, as soon as the dew had evaporated, we draped the long tables with white linen cloths and hung the garlands in large festoons around them. Then, we brought out the glasses and carafes, and polished the silver. We built pyramids of red apples and muscat grapes, using toothpicks to hold the apples together. All over the house people were busy arranging bouquets, breaking the iceblocks to chill the bottles which are in the fountain, and all of this amid laughter in the most organized havoc. The summer holidays are coming to an end, and we are going to hold a banquet in the garden as we have every year. The house is happy. Hordes of dogs and cousins are running everywhere. In the drawing room near the piano, like actors for a day, we are rehearsing the show that will be staged in the afternoon. In the linen room, final adjustments are being made to the costumes. In the kitchen, cooks are busy preparing the *aïoli*.

Wine cooling in the fountain

"Le Grand Aïoli"

~

WINE:
Côtes
du
Luberon
rosé

The *aïoli* can be a sauce or it can be the whole meal! The sauce with garlic and olive oil, strong and flavorful, is wonderful and a real taste of Provence. The meal can be a simple boiled dish, without meat, the kind of meal we would normally

eat on a Friday. But with the *aïoli* it is transformed into a magnificent feast.

IN THE KITCHEN : First you need a few large thick fillets of salt cod that have soaked in water for 24 hours, with at least 4 changes of water. When the salt has been removed, poach the fish for about 20 minutes, without letting it boil;

the water must barely simmer. You can serve the cod warm or cold.

Then prepare the vegetables: potatoes boiled in their skins and served hot; whole carrots, peeled and boiled; 1-2 small cauliflowers, nice and white, steamed until *al dente*; zucchini boiled in their skins; red beets, boiled then peeled; leeks, lightly boiled; green beans, blanched; and artichokes, boiled. Each vegetable must be cooked separately. You will also need hard-boiled eggs, which must be shelled before serving. Finally you need some snails that you will have fed with flour, to cleanse them, for 3 weeks prior to your feast. On the day, the snails should be poached for 20 minutes in salted water with a few herbs (some sprigs of thyme and 2 bay leaves).

Then you must prepare the sauce, in a large marble mortar with a wooden pestle. Mash a dozen garlic cloves until you get a smooth paste. Add 2 egg yolks which have been kept at room temperature. Work the *aïoli* like a mayonnaise, using a whisk instead of the pestle. Pour in the olive oil, which should be at room temperature too, little by little to begin with, and a little faster later, whisking all the time until the *aïoli* is thick and smooth. Add a touch of salt. That is all.

This is a very strongly flavored dish which can be accompanied equally well by red or rosé wine. It is, by definition, a summer feast, and could be sufficient on its own, but some finnicky eaters might balk at the idea. So, to please them as well, we have prepared other dishes, lighter and more conventional, but just as delicious and all equally suitable for serving at a garden feast.

Little Green Pies

~

It is necessary to start this dish by going for a walk. The wild herbs that you will collect on your country stroll will give your pies their distinctive green color. You can, of course, use only spinach or the green leaves of Swiss chard that you can buy at the market, but the pies will taste far better if you add some wild herbs such as arugula, tender dandelion leaves, young nettle shoots, gathered along the country lanes, and wild leeks that can be found growing in the vineyards.

Back in the kitchen, you will need to sort out and wash the herbs and spinach. Drain them well and chop coarsely. The ideal proportion is half spinach, half wild herbs. You can add a lettuce heart, which would give a delicate, slightly bitter flavor, and some herbs from the garden, but add these sparingly.

Pour a little olive oil into a large skillet over a low heat, and add the herb mixture. Allow the leaves and herbs to wilt slowly until all their water has evaporated and they are starting to dry out. Add some sea salt or Kosher salt and lots of freshly ground pepper. Let the herbs cool.

Meanwhile, make some puff pastry with 4 cups of all-purpose flour and 2 sticks (8 ounces) of butter, a little salt, and a little cold water. This will give you a fairly rough puff pastry; if you would like it to be richer, add more butter. Give it 4 turns, and roll it out to a ½ inch thick sheet. Then, cut out rectangles of pastry, measuring about 4 x 2½ inches. On half of the rectangles, place 1 tablespoon of the herb mixture, and then cover them with the other pastry rectangles, making sure to seal the edges completely, using a little water. With the tip of a knife, make a few slits in the pie crusts to decorate them, for example like the veins of a leaf. Brush with a little beaten egg yolk and cook in a fairly hot oven until they are puffed and golden. As with all puff pastry, these pies will be better served warm.

Eggplant à la Provençale or à la Bohémienne

~

Both these dishes consist of fried eggplant served cold with a good flavorful tomato *coulis*.

When you cut the eggplant lengthwise, the dish is called eggplant "*à la Provençale.*" When the eggplant are diced, it is called "*à la bohémienne.*"

IN THE KITCHEN : First, we are going to prepare the tomato *coulis*. Take some nice, ripe, red tomatoes; wash them, and cut them in quarters. Pour a little olive oil into a pan, heat it gently, and add the tomatoes, some sea salt or Kosher salt, a pinch of sugar, 2 garlic cloves, and a bouquet garni. Let the sauce simmer over a low heat, until the liquid from the tomatoes has evaporated and the sauce is nice and thick. Let it cool. If you want, you can strain the *coulis* through a fine strainer to make it smoother.

Now for the eggplants: wash and dry them, but do not peel them. Either slice them lengthwise, or dice them into ½ inch cubes. If you have time, sprinkle them with coarse sea salt or Kosher salt and leave for 2-3 hours, to let them release any excess water. The eggplant will then absorb less oil when you fry it. If you salt them, you will have to squeeze the water out by hand. Do not worry that they might be too salty.

Now you can then fry the eggplant pieces in a skillet in hot olive oil. As soon as they are golden-brown on all sides, remove them and let them drain on paper towels. When they are thoroughly drained, arrange the slices of eggplant on a platter around the tomato *coulis* and you have eggplant *à la Provençale*. Or mix the diced eggplant in just enough *coulis* to coat them and they are *à la bohémienne*.

Orange Tabbouleh and Eggplants à la Bohémienne

Ratatouille

~

Like the eggplant *à la Provençale* and *à la bohémienne*, ratatouille can be served cold, as a first course. Served hot, it is delicious with broiled lamb or rabbit with mustard.

First, we are going to prepare the vegetables. Wash and dry 4 large eggplants and 4 zucchini. Tail, but do not peel them. Dice them into ½ inch cubes. Wash and dry 2 large sweet red peppers, cut in half, remove the stalks, de-seed, core, and cut into pieces. Peel 5 very ripe tomatoes—it is easy to peel them if you first plunge them into a pan of boiling water for a few minutes—seed and dice them. Peel 5 white onions, and chop them roughly. You will also need 10 to 12 unpeeled garlic cloves.

Heat a little olive oil in a cast-iron pot over low heat. Fry the onions until they are soft and golden, then add the peppers and the eggplant cubes and let them brown to a nice golden color. Add the zucchini and let them brown a little too,

then the tomatoes, the garlic cloves, 1 bay leaf, a sprig of thyme, some sea salt or Kosher salt, freshly ground pepper, and 1 teaspoon of sugar. Stir thoroughly, and turn the heat up until the vegetables are simmering. Reduce the heat, cover and cook gently for 1 hour. After that time, remove the lid from the pot and continue cooking until all the excess liquid has evaporated.

Just before serving, add a minced garlic clove to the ratatouille. My grandmother Athalie used to call this "throwing in a touch of garlic." Stir the ratatouille and serve.

Omelet Gâteau
~

The omelet gâteau is served cold and sliced to show off its layers of pretty colors. If you have many guests, I suggest you make several small gâteaux instead of 1 large one.

Wine:
Côtes
du Luberon
rosé

Butter 1 large or several small, round-bottomed Pyrex dishes. In each you will stack 5 moist, creamy omelets of different flavors which will have been cooked one by one in a skillet with the same diameter as the chosen dish.

Start with a scallion omelet: cook 10 chopped scallions in a little olive oil over a low heat until they are soft and golden.

Take them out of the oil with a slotted spoon, and place them in a bowl with 6 eggs. Lightly beat with a fork and season with a pinch of sea salt or Kosher salt and freshly ground pepper. Heat the skillet and add a little more olive oil, if necessary. Pour in the eggs and stir gently with a wooden spoon. The skillet should be hot to begin with, but the omelet must be cooked over a low heat, because it must stay moist and should not change color. Do not flip the omelet over; slide it care-fully into the Pyrex dish, cooked-side down.

Omelet gâteau

*Pages 190-191:
Garden feast at the
Château de l'Ange in
Lumières*

Now for the spinach omelet: you will need a large handful of spinach, washed, chopped, and wilted in a little olive oil with salt and freshly ground pepper. Proceed as for the scallion omelet and when cooked, stack it in the Pyrex dish. The third omelet will be flavored with garlic: 1 garlic clove, finely chopped, is added to the eggs before beating. The fourth omelet is a tomato omelet: 2 large tablespoons of tomato *coulis* flavored with onion, garlic and thyme are added to the eggs before beating. In the last omelet, you will finely chop some parsley and chives. Bake the omelet gâteau in a bain-marie in a medium oven for 20 minutes. Then invert it on a dish and let it cool. This dish can be prepared the day before.

Bernard's Orange Tabbouleh

~

My friend Bernard is originally from Algiers, but Africa, the Orient, and Provence have long had very close ties. Everyone was used to seeing characters looking like the Wise Men from the Bible get off the boat at Marseilles harbor. The people of Provence were not fazed by their caftans, turbans, and spices. We were often the first in France to discover the strange and marvelous flavors brought in by the merchant ships which traded with Africa and the Middle East. Even today, in the rich markets of Provence, you will find turmeric and ginger, coriander, cinnamon, dried fruit, and pickled lemons from Morocco, their scents mingling naturally with those of basil and marjoram.

My friend Bernard is also a marvelous cook, when he sets his mind to it. He can, like no other, play around with the tastes and flavors of this mythical place he comes from. He has created this delicious tabbouleh with orange, cool and delicate, perfect for a summer lunch.

In THE KITCHEN : You will need to start the day before by peeling off the rind of 4 large oranges—but not the pith—and cutting it into very fine strips. Take a large, shallow, earthenware dish and place in it 8 cups of medium-grain couscous. Moisten it with the juice of 10 oranges and 4 lemons. Add the strips of orange rind and 1¼ cups of golden raisins. Mix well, cover the dish with aluminum foil and let it stand overnight.

The following day, crumble the couscous with your fingers to remove the lumps. Then add 1 bunch of flat-leaf parsley and the same quantity of mint leaves, finely chopped. Do not use a machine to chop the herbs, because this would produce an ugly brown purée that would spoil your tabbouleh. Peel, seed, and dice a few ripe tomatoes and 2 cucumbers. Add them to the couscous with some sea salt or Kosher salt, a generous pinch of freshly ground pepper, and a few tablespoons of olive oil. Mix thoroughly and store in a cool place for 1-2 hours before serving.

Joséphine Salad

~

Another exotic salad, named after the Empress who came from the islands. This salad is extremely simple and delicious: a handful of golden raisins, soaked for a few hours in the juice of 2 lemons; a cold cooked chicken, skinned, boned, and cut into pieces; a cold pork roast, cubed; a fresh coconut, cut into fine strips; the flesh of a grapefruit, cubed; a pinch of curry powder, a pinch of salt, and a generous dash of olive oil. Mix all the ingredients together, cover, and store in a cool place for at least 2 hours before serving.

WINE:
Condrieu

Curry and Condrieu, a perfect marriage

Mimosa Pastaga's
Sunshine Chicken

~

Mimosa Pastaga radiates warmth like the sun itself. The happy light in her eyes, the gaiety of her laughter, the generosity of her cooking, and the *joie de vivre* of her friends, always numerous at her table, are a delight to witness.

IN THE KITCHEN : The day before you want to cook the dish, prepare the marinade with 1 cup of olive oil, 1 tablespoon of sweet paprika, 1 tablespoon of turmeric, a pinch of sea salt or Kosher salt, and some freshly ground pepper. Cut 2 large chickens into pieces, place them in the marinade, turning the pieces to coat them in the spice mixture, and leave overnight in a cool place.

The following day, in a pan, brown the chicken in the oil from the marinade until nice and golden. Then remove the chicken. In the same pan, lightly brown 4 sliced onions, then add 6 crushed garlic cloves, and 4 large ripe tomatoes, peeled, seeded, and chopped. Add a piece of fresh ginger root and simmer for about 10 minutes. Return the chicken pieces to the pan and moisten with the juice of 2 lemons. Cook for a further 20 minutes over a low heat and add a few broken olives, purple and green. Let the olives heat through, then arrange the chicken in a large serving dish with some quartered pickled lemons. You will find these with the olives at most markets in Provence.

WINE :
Condrieu

Milk Gratin

~

This is the Provençal version of egg custard. Bring 1 quart of milk to a boil with 20 sugar cubes. Then let the milk cool slightly. Beat 6 or 7 eggs (depending on their size) with a fork and add 2 large tablespoons of rum. Mix the eggs into the warm milk and pour into a *tian* (gratin dish). Cook in a low oven for 30 minutes, or until the custard has set.

You can also caramelize the bottom of the *tian* (see recipe on page 120). Let the caramel harden before pouring in the egg and milk mixture. In this case, omit the rum. Serve warm or cold in the *tian*.

Mimosa Pastaga's
Sunshine Chicken

Chantilly Puffs

~

When I was a child, we would buy *petits choux* every Sunday morning at the bakers, and freshly made chantilly cream at the dairy. The chantilly cream was whipped on demand and only on Sunday mornings, with a huge noisy machine which worked with 2 large whisks. But what marvelous cream it was, and what a difference compared to those horrible cans of ready-made chantilly!

If you are in Provence, and if your local baker makes those little puffs called *bijoux de Nice*, and if your dairy whips up an authentic chantilly, then you do not need this recipe. But you will still enjoy filling the choux with cream. This was my job, and I am still licking my fingers. Just in case here goes . . .

In the Kitchen : In a saucepan, bring to the boil 1 pint of water, 1¾ sticks (7 ounces) of butter, 1 tablespoon of salt, and 2 tablespoons of sugar. When the mixture is boiling, add 3¼ cups of all-purpose flour all at once. Off the heat, beat vigorously with a wooden spoon until the paste stops sticking to the sides of the pan. Let the paste cool, then beat in 12 eggs, one by one. Using a pastry bag and nozzle, pipe your *petits choux* onto a buttered baking sheet and cook them for 30 minutes at 375°F. As soon as you take them out of the oven, sprinkle them with sugar crystals (if you get on well with your baker, he will probably let you have some). Let the choux cool completely and just before serving, fill them with good chantilly cream, either using a pastry bag or by slitting them through the middle. Any remaining choux can be used to make profiteroles.

To make a successful chantilly cream you will need 1 cup of *crème fleurette* (light cream) and 1 cup of *crème double* (thick heavy cream). Put them in the refrigerator for a few hours so they are cold. Of course, you will have chosen fresh, not sterilized cream. In a bowl, beat the creams, then whip them vigorously with a whisk until the chantilly is firm and frothy. Do not over-beat though, or it will turn to butter. Fold in 4 tablespoons of sugar and 2 teaspoons of vanilla sugar if available.

When wine colors sparkle in the sun

INDEX

~

acacia blossom fritters 108
"l'aïgo boulido" 61
aïoli, "le grand" 184-5
almonds: almond and anchovy
    sauce 127
    almond and garlic sauce 126
    black nougat 68-9
    calissons 69
    crunchy almond cookies 137
    my mother's almond log 75
anchovies: "l'anchoïade" 141
    anchovy quichets
      (toast) 126
    "brouffade" of the River Rhône 84
    a jar of anchovies 169
apples: caramel and apple cake 52
    simple apple pie 51
apricot gratin 181
artichokes: artichoke omelet 100
    artichoke salad 71
    artichokes "en barigoule" 104-6
    salad of purple artichokes 100
asparagus: truffles with Lauris 95
    wild asparagus omelet 95-6

beef: beef daube 148
    beef daube in jelly 145-6
    beef olives 85
    braised beef with carrots 81
    "brouffade" of the River Rhône 84
bouillabaisse 128-32
bread: olive bread 145
    Orange fougasse 68
brouffade of the River Rhône 84
"brouillade" with truffles 78

cabbage: La potée d'amour 36
    large and small stuffed
      cabbages 23
cakes: Auntie Lilette's strawberry
    cake 107-8
    caramel and apple cake 52
    chocolate cake 52
    fruit cake 48-50
    golden raisin cake 50-1

honey spice cake 53
my cousin Jeanne's saint-honoré
    40-2
my mother's almond log 75
my strawberry cake 107
Nanie's cake 148
orange cake 53
pear cake 28
calissons 69
candied peel, orange and lemon 31
"capon," stuffed 133
cardoon tian 62-5
"Carthagène" 121
celeriac purée 87
celery with anchovies 61
chantilly puffs 196
cheese: Brousse cheese from
    Rove 165
    cheese ravioli 101
    goats' cheese in olive oil 40
    "lou cachat" 119
cherry clafoutis 149
chicken: Mimosa Pastaga's
    sunshine 195
    poached chicken 72
chickpeas, "baïano" of 74
chocolate: chocolate cake 52
    hot chocolate 48
clams, spaghetti with 162
cod: salt cod, Grandet style 158
    salt cod with leeks 66-7
    creamed salt cod tian 67
    "le grand aïoli" 184-5
    my mother's salt cod gratin 173
    salt cod bouillabaisse 131-2
coffee: my mother's almond log 75
cookies: crunchy almond
    cookies 137
    little vanilla crescents 56
    navettes 162-3
    rock cookies 136
custard: snow cream 133-6
cuttlefish: fisherman's "rouille"
    114-16

daube from Avignon 80-1
dried fruit compote, Véronique L.'s
    90

eggplant: "à la provençale" 186-7
    broiled peppers and eggplant 119
    glazed eggplant tian 174
    Jérôme's eggplant stew 117
    Madame Cheynet's eggplants
      174-6
eggs: "brouillade" with truffles 78
    egg soup 78
    stuffed eggs 79
    see also omelets
endive compote 86

fennel: and tomatoes 158
    my godmother Lilou's compote 85
figs: fig gratin 181
    fig jam 165
fish: bouillabaisse 128-32
flowers, sugar 42
fougasse, Orange 68
fritters: acacia blossom 108
    Madame Pavan's "oreillettes" 89
    zucchini and zucchini-blossom
      168-9
fruit cake 48-50

golden raisin cake 50-1
grapes in eau-de-vie 70

honey spice cake 53

jam: fig 165
    green tomato 33
    rose-hip 55
    watermelon 121

kid, roast with anchovy 102

lamb: daube from Avignon 80-1
    leg with garlic cream sauce 102
    trotters and tripe bundles 178-9

lentils, New Year's Day 72-4
"lou cachat" 119

marmalade, bitter orange 55-6
meat: meat ravioli 101
    le pot-au-feu 37
"meissounenco à la sucarello" 113-14
milk gratin 195
morels with pork sausages 104
mussels, ravioli with 101

navettes 162-3
nougat, black 68-9

octopus: spaghetti "au monstre" 161
olives: broken olives 112
    olive bread 145
    pricked olives 112-13
    tapenade 125-6
omelets: artichoke 100
    irreplaceable tomato 140
    omelet gâteau 188-92
    wild asparagus 95-6
Oraison gratin 27
Orange fougasse 68
oranges: Bernard's tabbouleh 192-3
    bitter orange marmalade 55-6
        Edith's orange and caramel
        salad 88
    orange and lemon candied peel 31
    orange cake 53
    orange wine 168
"oreillettes," Madame Pavan's 89

pasta: lumache pasta salad 146-8
pear cake 28
peppers, broiled eggplants and 119
persimmons with rum 30
pies: spinach and pignoli pie 62
    simple apple pie, 51
pork: Catherine's roast with
    sage 38-9
    Oraison gratin 27
Le pot-au-feu 37
potatoes: baked potatoes 26
    celeriac purée 87
    the Countess' potatoes 106
    fisherman's "rouille" 114-16

French fries, Vinsobres style 154
    mashed potatoes with leeks 86
    Oraison gratin 27
    a picturesque salad 117
    potatoes and spinach tian 80
    potatoes with bacon 26
"poutargue," 125
pumpkin: pumpkin and bread
    soup 20
    pumpkin and rice tian 22
    pumpkin and spinach tian 21-2
    stuffed pumpkin 21

quince paste, Auntie Lilette's 27-8

rabbit: garlic rabbit 24
    rabbit sausage with olives 144
    rabbit terrine 141-4
    with mustard sauce 24
radish greens or nettle soup 173
ratatouille 187-8
ravioli: fried ravioli 127
    homemade ravioli 100-1
rice: Annie Laurent's rice
    pudding 120
    Rosette's rice pudding 87
rose-hip jam 55
rouille 129
"rouille," fisherman's 114-16

le saint-honoré 40-2
salads: fisherman's "rouille" 114-16
    green salad 96
    Joséphine salad 193
    lumache pasta salad 146-8
    a picturesque salad 117
    purple artichokes 100
    small salads 39
sauces: almond and anchovy 127
    almond and garlic 126
    l'anchoïade 141
    sauce rouge 38
    sauce vert 38
sausages, morels with pork 104
sea bream, the baron's 157
sea urchin "rouille" 129
sea urchins 153
shortbread 136

snails: "meissounenco à la sucarello"
    113-14
snow cream 133-6
soups: "l'aïgo boulido" 61
    Auntie Lilette's "soupe au pistou"
    172
    egg soup 78
    pumpkin and bread soup 20
    radish greens or nettle soup 173
spaghetti: Auntie Anne's 162
    spaghetti "au monstre" 161
    spaghetti with clams 162
spice cake cream, Véronique L.'s 90
spinach: spinach and pignoli pie 62
    spinach and sardine tian 79
strawberry cakes 107-8
sugar flowers 42

tapenade 125-6
"tellines à l'aïoli" 116
thirteen desserts 70
toffee, my grandmother's Russian
    31-3
tomatoes: green tomato jam 33
    irreplaceable tomato omelet 140
    tomato coulis 159-61
    tomato preserve 159
    tomatoes à la provençale 179
truffles: "brouillade" with 78
    Lauris asparagus with 95
    truffle stew 65-6

vanilla crescents 56
vegetables: little green pies 185-6
    les petits farcis 176-7
    stew of spring vegetables 103

walnut wine, Olga's 168
watermelon jam 121
wine: "Carthagène" 121
    Olga's walnut wine 168
    orange wine 168

zucchini: zucchini gratin 176
    fritters 168-9

ACKNOWLEDGEMENTS

~

It was while we were having dinner at home, in the kitchen with the *cicadas*, that Jean-Pierre and Christine Deméry convinced me to write this book, and today I am delighted to thank them for this excellent idea. My grandmother, my mother, my aunt Elisabeth, Mamie Rosette and Madame Cheynet, my cousin Jeanne and my godmother Louise have taught me everything I know. And I love them. But it is from my father, a hunter, a trout fisherman, a connoisseur of wine and good food, a man who could tell you stories about memorable meals that would make you drool, that I have inherited this passion for food, this pleasure in eating well, without which this book would probably never have been written.

My friends, Edith Mézard, Elisabeth Bourgeois, Martine Albertin, Lydie Laurent and Françoise Quinta, Monique and Jean-Claude Duveau, Annie Laurent, Véronique Lopez, Bruno Vaïarelli, Jo Guesde, Bernard Paul, Gérard Drouillet, "Queen Jeanne," Eliane Jouve, Thierry Guien and Anne Sportiello, Hélène Feraud and Simone Rossi, Jérôme Couturier and Françoise de la Brosse, Thérèse Pavan, Françoise and Lionel Guin, have all frequently entertained me at their table, before and during the preparation of this book. They have been its inspiration and its pleasure. I thank them.

My friends Ted and Lillian Williams, Jacques Grange, Géraud and Stéphanette de Sabran, Henri and Annie Laurent, Jean-Baptiste and Nicole Juge, Jean and Hélène Féraud, Michel and Edith Mézard, Bruno Carles, Gérard Drouillet, and Denis Savon have been generous enough to lend me the enchanting places where we took the photographs for this book.

It is hard to imagine the cataclysm that strikes a house when a team of photographers and stylists arrive. The furniture is piled up in the corridors, some windows are darkened with cloth while others are enhanced with silver reflectors. The floor is suddenly covered with crumpled bits of paper. Often, while you are shooting a lunch scene in the sun, nature gets in the way, clouds darken the sky so you have to bring out all the spotlights and their cables get merrily entangled. In the middle of all this mayhem, within the frame determined by Bernard Touillon's shrewd eye, the picture is being slowly organized, a picture which does not appear very clear to the untrained eye. I thank all my friends for their patience and their trust, and I hope Bernard's beautiful photographs will have totally reassured them by now.

How could I forget to thank Ariane and Gérard Blanc for letting me use their lovely yellow china for so long, as well as Bernard Paul and Bruno Carles of *l'Espace Béchard*, and Maria Giancatarina and Jean-Claude Clément of the Quai de la Gare in l'Isle-sur-la-Sorgue who kindly lent me part of their collections, and of course, my dear Edith Mézard who, often at the last minute, embroidered, sewed or ironed the tablecloths used for this book.

My thanks to Philippe Baique, wine waiter at the *Mas de Tourteron* in Gordes, who advised me so cleverly about the choice of wines.

I certainly would not want to forget Francette Drin who has been so helpful with her kind and thoughtful advice. Thanks to her, this book has gained its clarity.

Finally, this book has taken shape thanks to the experience and the talent of Ghislaine Bavoillot, Marc Walter, and Florence Picard.